Never Let Me Down

Henry Holt and Company
New York

Never Let Me Down

A   M E M O I R

Susan J. Miller

Thanks to Bill Buford, Darcy Tromanhauser,
and Jennifer Unter.

Henry Holt and Company, Inc.
Publishers since 1866
115 West 18th Street
New York, New York 10011

Henry Holt® is a registered trademark of
Henry Holt and Company, Inc.

Library of Congress Cataloging-in-Publication Data
Miller, Susan J., date.
Never let me down: a memoir / Susan J. Miller.—1st ed.
    p.   cm.
ISBN 0-8050-4429-9 (hardcover: alk. paper)
1. Children of narcotic addicts—United States—Case studies.
2. Narcotic addicts—United States—Family relationships—Case
    studies. 3. Miller, Susan J., date.   I. Title.
HV5824.C45M55   1998   97-13690
362.29'33—dc21   CIP

Henry Holt books are available for special promotions and
premiums. For details contact: Director, Special Markets.

First Edition 1998

Designed by Kate Nichols

Printed in the United States of America
All first editions are printed on acid-free paper. ∞
        3   5   7   9   10   8   6   4   2

Parts of this book first appeared in slightly altered
form in *Granta* Number 47 and *Harper's*.

This book is dedicated to my friends,
past and present,
to my mother,
and to Max, Eleanor, and Maury

But especially it is for my dear doctors,
Millicent Dewar and Jane Bain,
without whom . . .

Memory is a kind of accomplishment.

—William Carlos Williams

Never Let Me Down

I

One night, at an hour that was normally my bedtime, I got all dressed up, and my mother and father and I drove into New York, down to the Half Note, the jazz club on Hudson Street. I was thirteen, maybe fourteen, just beginning teenagehood, and had never gone anywhere that was "nightlife." I had heard jazz all my life, on records or on the radio, my father beating out time on the kitchen table, the steering wheel, letting out a breathy "Yeah" when the music soared and flew. When they were cooking, when they really swung, it transported him; he was gone, inside the music. I couldn't go on this trip with him, but I thought I could understand it. It seemed to me that anyone could, hearing that music. Bird, Diz, Pres, Sweets, Lester, Al, Zoot. It was my father's music, though he himself never played a note.

I knew the players, for about the only friends my parents had were musicians and their wives. When I was a little kid, I'd

lie in bed listening to them talk their hip talk in the next room.
I knew I was the only kid in Washington Heights to be over-
hearing words like *man* and *cat* and *groove*, and jokes that were
this irreverent and black. I knew they were cool and I loved it.

At the Half Note that night, the three of us walked through
the door, and the owner appeared, all excited to see my father,
and, in the middle of this smoky nightlife room, he kissed my
hand. This was real life, the center of something. We sat down.
In front of us, on a little stage, were Jimmy Rushing, a powerful
singer, and two sax players, Al Cohn and Zoot Sims, whom I'd
known all my life. And there was a whole *roomful* of people
slapping the tables, beating out time, breathing "Yeah" at the
great moments, shaking their heads, sometimes snapping their
fingers, now and then bursting out with "Play it, man," or
"Sing it." When the break came, Zoot sat down with us and
ate a plate of lasagna or something and didn't say much except
for these dry asides that were so funny I couldn't bear it. Too
funny to laugh at. And there was my dad: these men were his
friends, his buddies. They liked the things about my father that
I could like—how funny he was, uncorny; how unsentimental,
unafraid to be different from anyone else in the world: how he
was unafraid to be on the edge.

As a child, I didn't know that my father and many of the
musicians who sat with their wives in our living room, eating
nuts and raisins out of cut-glass candy dishes, were junkies. It
wasn't until I was twenty-one, a college senior, that my father
told me that he had been a heroin addict, casually slipping that
information into some otherwise unremarkable conversation.
The next day my mother filled in the story. My father had
begun shooting up in 1946, when my mother was pregnant

with my brother, who is nineteen months older than I am. My father stopped when I was around thirteen and my brother was fifteen—the same age as my father's addiction.

I never suspected a thing. Nor did my brother. We never saw any drug paraphernalia. There was a mysterious purplish spot in the crook of my father's elbow, which he said had something to do with the army. His vague explanation was unsatisfactory, but even in my wildest imaginings I never came near the truth. In the 1950s, in the white, middle- and working-class communities where we lived, no one discussed drugs, which were synonymous with the utmost degradation and depravity. My parents succeeded in hiding my father's addiction from us, but, as a result, we could never make sense of the strained atmosphere, our family's lack of money, our many moves. The addiction was the thread that tied everything together. We didn't know that such a thread existed, and so decisions seemed insanely arbitrary, my mother's emotions frighteningly hysterical. My father was often away, staying out late or not coming home at all. My brother and I fought often and violently. My mother was terribly depressed, sometimes desperate. I regularly found her sitting, eyes unfocused, collapsed amid the disorder of a household she was too overwhelmed to manage. She would beg my father not to go out at night. As I got older, I tried to figure out what was going on. An affair? This was a logical explanation, but it didn't fit.

My father was a man of socially unacceptable habits. He was fat, he picked his teeth, he burped, he farted, he blew his nose into the sink in the morning, he bit his nails until he had no nails and then he chewed his fingers, eating himself up. He was a high-octane monologuer, a self-taught high school dropout who constantly read, thought, and talked politics and culture, gobbling up ideas, stuffing himself as fast as he could—with everything.

He was from Brighton Beach, Brooklyn, and earned his living dressing windows in what were called "ladies' specialty shops"—independently owned women's clothing stores in and around New York City. He went from store to store in his display-laden station wagon, visiting the shops every month or so when they changed their windows. Being a window dresser was a touch creative, but, most important, it meant he didn't have to fit in; all he had to do was get the job done.

How did a bright Jewish boy from Brighton Beach become a junkie in the late 1940s? It was partly the crowd he hung out with: white musicians deeply under the influence of Charlie Parker—and Parker's drug, heroin. Stan Getz, Al Cohn, George Handy—all were junkies and all were my father's friends.

My father began with marijuana at age fifteen. Although he was drafted during the Second World War, he never made it overseas; he was, I was told, "honorably discharged" from boot camp in Georgia for health reasons: he was deemed too weak to fight, having lost weight because of the heat. I've always found the story rather odd, if only because, in the army pictures I've seen, he looks so happy and active, even if a little thin, clowning in front of the camera with his friends. Perhaps the story is true, but it seems unlikely. By his late twenties, he was a heroin addict. Ten years later, he was taking amphetamines as well. He occasionally gave me some when I was in college to help me stay up all night writing papers; they were very strong. When he was about fifty, though no longer on heroin, he was taking LSD, mescaline, peyote, whatever he could get.

At college I received long letters from him, written when he was coming down from an acid or mescaline trip. Often he tripped alone in the living room of my parents' New Jersey apartment, awake all night, listening to records, writing and thinking while my mother slept. I read pages of his blocky, slanted printing, about how the world is a boat and we are all sinking. So many pages with so many words. Usually I threw them away without finishing them, scanning his stoned raps in front of the big green metal trash can in the college mail room, picturing him in the living room with the sun rising, wired up, hunched over the paper, filling up the page, wanting me to know all the exciting things he had discovered. Part of me wanted to hear about them and love him—and indeed I did love him for taking the acid, for taking the chance. But another part shut down, unable to care. I would look out of the mail room window onto the college's perfect green lawn, scenic mountains in the distance, little white houses with green shutters, the place of my willed exile, my escape.

One day when I was home from college on vacation, my father and I went into New York together. He was going to retrieve his car from a garage in the West Forties, take me to a friend's downtown, and then pick up my mother at her midtown office and drive her home. We took the bus across the bridge, then got on the subway at 178th Street. After the doors shut, my father edged close to me, putting his mouth up to my ear to make himself heard over the screech of the train. I took acid before we left the house this morning and I'm just starting to get off, he said. He was smiling, a naughty kid out in the big grown-up world. My heart sank. My father had swallowed a psychic explosive that might detonate him and then me, if his trip turned bad. The train rocked furiously back and forth, its lights flickering, racing at sixty miles an hour through its pitch-black tunnel on the longest nonstop run in the city, from 125th Street to 59th Street. At any moment the subway car might turn into a sealed tomb on an endless nightmare ride. Acid makes you vulnerable, a sponge. It would take only seconds, a quick switch in his head, and he would be gripping my arm and saying, Susan, I've got to get out of here. Now, right now.

We reached our stop, and I stayed close, following him through the smelly, mobbed, low-ceilinged station, where at every turn I saw something I feared might set him off: glistening hot dogs revolving under infrared lights; a legless man on a wheeled board, selling pencils. But at the garage my father understood the Puerto Rican mechanic's broken English better than I did. He checked the itemized bill and counted out dollars and coins the right way the first time. Last time I took acid, I found myself in a little family grocery in Santa Fe, staring dumbfounded at the meaningless disks of silver in my hand, unable to buy an orange Popsicle without help, thunderstruck by the very concept of money, its simultaneous brilliance and folly. My dad was having no such problems. He was energized; he was having fun. He got behind the wheel and headed out into the river of cars, the honking, swerving cabs, the sticky stop-and-go jams. He dropped me off, waved good-bye, headed back uptown to pick up my mother.

Watching him trip was like discovering that your father was an accomplished deep-sea diver or high-wire artist. Yet I knew that even the best tightrope walker slips. I limped up to my friend's, exhausted.

Never marry a musician, my mother admonished me when I was growing up—in the same way, I suppose, that other mothers warned their daughters off criminals or *shvartzers* or Jews. I suspected she had a point; life married to a man always on the road would be no picnic. I had heard about the hotel rooms and buses and daytime sleeping. I also knew she meant something more complex—that these men were not to be trusted. She could say, Don't marry one, because she had seen so many. What she didn't say, and what I didn't know, was that so many were junkies. Because I didn't know what lay behind her warnings, they seemed mysteriously exaggerated.

The musicians who came to our house fascinated me; their pants with black satin stripes down the sides, their hipster banter, their battered horn cases. My father could hear anyone on the radio and know who was playing. He'd say, That's Pres, or, Listen to Diz swing. I loved the fame of these men, the fact that the world knew their names, their sounds, that there were pictures of them in *Down Beat*. I knew some, like Al and Zoot, but most of them I'd never met. They were part of the life my father lived away from us children. To me these were names, or sounds on records, or sometimes faces in our photo album; they belonged to men leaning against lampposts in the Village, or sitting with their arms around attractive women on rocks in Central Park. Allen Eager, Tiny Kahn, George Handy, Stan Getz, Johnny Mandel, Georgie Auld—these names resonate in my heart like the Yiddish that I heard so often then.

I don't know what went on between my father and these men. All I know is that for my father, his junkie years were the greatest of his life. He wanted to tell me about them, so I would understand why he wasn't sorry about what he had done. He wanted me to know about the great and wild people he had met, the music he had heard, the crazy underworld places he had been to. He needed to explain that, while being a junkie sounded bad to other people, it had been really wonderful for him. But I couldn't listen. For me those years of his heroin addiction had been a time of fearful poverty, violence at the hands of my brother, and terror that my mother would cease to function. No, I said, I don't want to hear. Each of us was furious: my worst times were his best.

In 1973, two years after my father told me about his addiction, he stopped in to visit me at my apartment on Charlton Street. He was distraught, not an unusual state for him. *Damaged merchandise,* he said, are the words I see in front of me when things get bad, and when I see those words, I know it's all over. Do you understand that? He fixed me with his wild, wide-open, hazel eyes. Do you understand what I am trying to say?

Yes, I said, over and over. Yes, I understand what you are trying to say, but I knew he could scarcely see or hear me through the haze and buzz of electric cloud around his head.

Damaged merchandise. He was a window dresser; he spent hours making signs on thick white rectangular cards with a creamy-smooth surface, writing them out in front of the television the night before the job. SALE, they said, HANES HOSIERY, $1.99 A PAIR, or whatever. The next day he propped the signs up in front of the displays, a bra folded carefully, skillfully, and laid out on the floor, cups pointing up and out. Stockings draped over the Lucite stand, the card tipped in front. At Christmas he piled mounds of fake snow, hung tinsel, attached big red bows, positioned empty packages wrapped in foil paper, red and green and silver. In the summer there were palm trees and beach balls. He was the window dresser, his station wagon filled with displays and rolls of no-seam paper, sprays of stiff flowers; thick cotton sockettes over his shoes to protect the floor, eyes bugged out, seeing in his mind's eye *himself*, on sale, marked down, damaged merchandise, an item nobody, not even the most inveterate bargain hunter, would want.

And he told me this, he spelled it out for me, and I listened even though I didn't want to. I hadn't yet learned how to tell him no; I still thought it was my job to listen to what anyone in my family wanted to say to me: as I had when my brother told me his sexual fantasies, or when my mother told me how horrible she felt about herself and us. My father paced around my living room, his voice ranting, careening, echoing in the big empty room that was his sad and lonely and frightened heart. It scared me to listen, because I knew that I had been damaged, too: by his not seeing me, as he was not seeing me right then. The room was turning into a funnel, and I felt myself being sucked down into it. I acted very polite, trying to remain a whole person. I asked him some questions. I tried to change the subject. And then I don't remember what I did. Maybe I yelled at him, or maybe I just asked him to leave, telling him I had to go somewhere. Or maybe I said, Oh, Daddy, it's awful you feel that way. I was trying to hold on to myself, and no response I could choose would have been any better than any other. Nothing woke him up to me.

In December 1988, I went to visit my father, who at age seventy was dying of liver cancer in the two-bedroom apartment in Fort Lee, New Jersey, that he called his little white box. He and my mother had been living in this apartment since I was a freshman in high school. Like all our apartments, this one hadn't had enough bedrooms. At first my brother slept on the foldout couch in the living room and kept his things in the bedroom where I slept, but after he graduated from high school and moved out, two years after we had moved in, I had the bedroom to myself, as well as a bathroom. My parents had their own bathroom off their bedroom, and there was a large living room, a tiny dinette, and a minuscule kitchen. It was the nicest apartment we had lived in. The building was fairly new when we moved in, not more than eight years old. Our apartment had thick, solid walls, and the beams and supports jutted out but were plastered over, so that the apartment had a white-washed, Mediterranean feel. From one of the living room windows you could glimpse a sliver of the Hudson River through the thick woods that edged the Palisades.

I had lobbied heavily for us to move to this apartment. My mother was reluctant. She liked it but was concerned about affording the rent, which was higher than we had ever paid. I didn't at the time know why our economic situation had recently improved to the point that we could even consider such an upgrade in our living conditions. Unbeknownst to me, my father had stopped using heroin, but I suppose my mother couldn't be certain his habit was permanently over. As it turned out, it was, and the terrible feeling of being inches from utter destitution ceased being a constant in our lives.

My father's liver cancer had developed as a consequence of hepatitis B, which he had contracted from needles at some point during the fifteen or so years he was shooting up. Until his liver cancer was discovered that August, during routine gallbladder surgery, no one, including my father, had ever known that he had the virus. He had been asymptomatic, as many people are. The virus affects the liver; primary liver cancer is unusual, except in junkies, since hepatitis B is pretty well relegated to that portion of the population. In my father's case, the hepatitis had been working on his liver in secret for something like forty years. When the surgeon opened him up, he saw that the liver was almost destroyed. He told my mother that my father could live about five months more, an estimate that turned out to be correct.

My mother called me and told me about the cancer and the five months to live. My husband, Maury, who is a family doctor, explained to me the relationship between hepatitis B and liver cancer. Ultimately, then, it was his addiction that was killing him, and every time this thought entered my mind, a frisson would go through me. No matter how often I'd think it, I'd feel this thrill. It had to do with some deep-down part of me that had never believed he had been a junkie, that had kept the story dreamlike and doubtful. After all, when it was happening, I hadn't known about it. Now the cancer and the hepatitis proved to me it had been real. So it's true, I'd say to myself, he really was a junkie.

I couldn't believe that things had worked out so fittingly. My father insisted that his addiction had had no serious consequences for anyone, that it was over and done with in every way. He was the only one of us who believed he had gotten off scot-free. My mother, brother, and I, all in our different ways, knew we were struggling with the legacy of his addiction. The joke, if you could have called it that, was that the heroin had been living on in him all the years he had been denying that it had consequences. Now the cancer had somewhat evened the score. The drug had affected us all, but it was killing him. That poetic justice was part of the thrill I kept feeling.

There had been hints that my father was sick, but we didn't know what they meant. A few years ago he started to look a little ashen, unhealthy. He was tired all the time. He would come to our house to visit and spend the day sleeping on the couch. He no longer went into New York to see movies or to go to museums with my mother. He stopped doing almost everything. His doctors blamed his weight and his age. He went on a liquid diet, lost fifty pounds, but was still tired and gray.

He came up to visit us when he was on that diet, carrying his cans of Optifast shake in a plastic shopping bag. When he was hungry, he'd get out the blender and mix himself a batch. He told me: You know what Dave Allen said to me the other day? He saw me drinking this stuff, and he said, Hey, Sidney, kicking again? My father laughed. Dave had also been a junkie. It took me a second to get it, then I laughed, too.

Immediately after the diagnosis he felt no different physically; he still had the same fatigue. By October he was in pain. He tried various remedies, including a macrobiotic diet and chemotherapy. He enrolled in an experimental cancer treatment program in New Haven but had to drop out because he soon became too weak to make the trip.

In November when I saw him, he was eager to share his latest revelation with my mother and me. A social worker in the experimental treatment program had asked him what he would miss most when he died. It was an interesting question, and I was interested to hear his answer. He said: I told her that, yeah, sure, I'll miss my wife and kids, but what I'll miss most is the music. The music is the only thing that's never let me down.

That this revelation would hurt us—especially my mother, who had stuck by him through everything—never occurred to him. He never kept his thoughts to himself, even if it was cruel to express them. Neither my mother nor I said a word. The statement was the truth of him—not only what he said but also the fact that he would say it to us, and say it without guilt, without apology, without regret.

After my father got too sick to drive up to Yale, my mother made arrangements to take care of him at home, with the support of a hospice program. The agency provided some help, but mostly she'd been nursing him on her own. Lately he'd been in increasing pain. Shortly after Maury and I arrived, she took me aside in the living room, out of his hearing: Those pills make him like the old Sidney, she burst out, terribly upset. It took me a second to realize that she meant the morphine pills the doctor had prescribed for pain. My mother, who never did anything more than get giggly once in a blue moon on a little wine at dinner and hadn't smoked cigarettes even in the days when no one knew they could kill you, had such bad memories that she hated to give him his morphine pills—more than hated to, could barely stand to, had to force herself to pick up the bottle and tip out a pill and watch him swallow it.

It was like asking the wife of an ex-alcoholic to hold a glass of whiskey to her husband's lips. The doctor had clearly never thought of this, though by now he knew my father's history. This drug could never be just medicine to my mother. The Sidney stoned on hash or grass or even the tripping Sidney, that's not the one she hated. She hated the heroin-drugged Sidney. When he takes those pills, he's back, the old Sidney; I never wanted to see him again, she said vehemently. She looked old and exhausted and near the breaking point. My heart seized up: Would she be able to continue caring for him? Compassion in her always was stronger than anger. She couldn't stand to see him suffer. She gave him the pills and would keep on giving them, even though for her it was a nightmare.

My mother said that all kinds of terrible memories had been flooding back, overwhelming her. After a pill, she said, the changes in his eyes, his speech, just the whole way he looked and talked, brought her back to those days. She explained to me apologetically, You probably wouldn't even notice anything much different in him, they are subtle things, but to me it's plain as day. The changes are obvious if you've been around it a lot.

She said she was ashamed for not wanting to give him the pills. She felt selfish. She knew she had no choice; it was medicine.

My mother and I stood in the living room on the red-patterned rug. She was so small, so drooping. A tired woman, strong and weak. There was nothing I could do but say small words. Oh, Mom, it must be hard.

Maury was in the bedroom, most likely asking my father, in his kindly doctor way, how he was doing this morning. Maury had a way of talking to my father that openly acknowledged the fact that he was dying and at the same time was pleasant and relaxed, almost bantering. It was the most comforting voice I could imagine. Being a family doctor, Maury had had plenty of practice talking to the dying. I had never been near a dying person before. This now struck me as unbelievable. I wasn't afraid. But I was puzzled. How could it be that I had never seen anyone at death's door? All you had to do was take a look at my father and it was obvious he was dying. His face was further transforming into a skeleton each day, not just from skinniness but as a harbinger of a state he was growing into. He had started to look plainly like death even a couple of months ago, when he was still walking around on his own. I must have passed a man in a wheelchair with that look or a woman on a park bench, sometime in my adult life.

I thought about all the people who died every day, all the thousands of people who were dying right at that moment.

People were dying in hospitals and nursing homes and in their own houses every minute, every second. The world was filled all the time with dying people, it was buzzing with death, and I had never seen it. I had been shielded from death by closed doors. It was like labor. The only people who get to see child-birth are the coaches, the caregivers; the rest of us never know what it looks like until there we are on the bed ourselves, sweating and screaming and pushing. Now was my chance to see death. And I was lucky. I wasn't sad my father was dying, I wasn't going to try to hold on to him, as I would if Maury were dying. I wasn't facing a loss that would devastate my life.

We had arrived from Cambridge the previous afternoon, with Max, who was two, and Eleanor, who was five. Jews tradi-tionally name a child after a deceased family member, by using either a relative's first name itself or its initial. Max had been named after my mother's father, Maximilian Berman, and my father's father, Maximilian Miller. This made both of my par-ents happy; they wanted to honor their fathers, even though Max Berman had been harsh and Max Miller had been distant. It was a different story with Eleanor. *E* was the first letter of Maury's grandfather's name, Eli, but it was also the initial of my father's terrible mother. You can name her Eleanor, said my mother, but only if we agree, and she knows when she is older, that she is not named after Esther.

When we all trooped into the apartment, my father hobbled out of the bedroom into the living room, leaning on his rented walker, and lowered himself slowly, carefully, into a chair. He sat with us for an hour, not saying much, mostly beaming at Max and Eleanor. At one point he gestured across the room to the copper-lined stereo cabinet built by my brother, which glowed golden inside, and asked Maury to put on an album that was on the turntable. It was an old Al Cohn and Zoot Sims record. He told us that lately he had been listening to no music but theirs. That was all he wanted to hear, that and some Charlie Parker. His good friend Al had died of liver cancer only a few months before. Al's wife, Flo, had been working, for the past few years, on setting some of my father's poems to music, and the four of them had often spent weekends together at the Cohns' house in the Poconos. In 1985, Zoot also died of liver cancer, caused in his case by alcoholism.

We spent the night at Maury's sister's apartment in Manhattan. Lying in bed, the children finally asleep, we discussed the day. Maury told me that when he was helping him back to bed, he asked my father what instrument he would have liked to play. Maury plays sax and clarinet, and he and my father would listen to records whenever we got together, my father tapping his foot and slapping his knee, Maury with his head tipped slightly to one side, his bright eyes twinkling with pleasure. Maury had expected my father to say the sax, which is what I would have expected, too, but he said the drums.

This really surprised us, since my father most admired the sax players, and we stayed awake for a while talking about it. Maybe he would have been a good drummer and maybe not. He had lots of talents milling around inside him, unrealized, and maybe drumming had been one of them. Until he started writing poems when he was in his late fifties, he hadn't homed in on any of them, hadn't turned any of them into skills or even hobbies. The very idea of a hobby would have filled him with scorn. Hobbyists were dull people who collected coins or made spice racks. He listened to music passionately, he read insatiably, but these were necessities, not hobbies. He had, all his life, appreciated, received, greedily, voraciously, but he had not created. The fact that over the course of fifteen years he had written a small body of poems, and that these poems had been read and enjoyed by others, was an absolute amazement to him. He wasn't bitter that he hadn't accomplished more. He was still dazzled that he accomplished something at all.

In the morning Maury and I went back to Fort Lee without the children. I brought along my suitcase. Yesterday it had looked to Maury as if my father would live only a few days longer, maybe a week. I was going to stay with my mother and help her take care of my father until he died.

Heading to Fort Lee, we drove over the George Washington Bridge in the early morning, against the traffic. The Hudson was gray and choppy. I loved the river. In the winter it sometimes had chunks of gray-white ice floating on the surface, broken up and banging against one another. Sometimes the river was blue and smooth. Sometimes it sparkled. When I was little, people in Fort Lee still caught shad in it. My best friend Debbie's brothers went down to the river every spring to catch the shad. I had never heard of shad or roe. There were animals on the Palisades in those days. Debbie's brother Timmy saw a bear one day, walking out of the woods. It seems like ancient history, bears on the cliffs and shad in the water.

Looking at the river made me sad. It had made my heart ache when I was young, too, but in those days I was sad so often that anything eternal filled me with longing. Maybe what was getting to me now were old memories of looking at the river, tears choking up my throat. But just as it had then, looking at the river also helped. It was an old friend, bigger and stronger than I was, reliable, majestic. It had been gouged out by a glacier; Indians paddled on it; Henry Hudson tasted it for salt, thinking he had found the Northwest Passage; Jerseyites ferried across it before the bridge was built. People did all kinds of things on it and to it, but it kept on filling with waves and ice and sloshing against the rocks on its shores.

Maury joined my mother and me in the living room. Sidney wants to talk to you, he said to me, and sat down with my mother. I headed to the bedroom on the hard floor, concrete covered with wooden parquet, so it never creaked or had any bounce. My parents' bed had been moved to my old room and replaced with a rented hospital bed, where my father lay. Except to go to the bathroom that afternoon, he would not get out of bed again. By the next day he would be using a bedpan. The head of the bed had been cranked up about 45 degrees, to a position between sitting up and lying down. When he turned to look at me, I saw a face that was dramatically more cadaverous than it had been yesterday: my father's eyes further sunken and darker, his facial bones even more prominent through his jaundiced, yellow-green skin. His arms and neck seemed skinnier, his legs and feet even more grotesquely swollen. When he shifted his legs under the covers, I could see his shiny skin, stretched to the limit.

In August, when I heard he was going to die, I didn't rush off to New Jersey. By then I hadn't seen my father for nearly a year, which had been, all things considered, a great relief. It felt like a vacation, I said to friends, like going to the beach and lying in the sun. Relaxing, wonderful. Would I see him ever again? I couldn't be sure. Things between us had been so bad for so long, and the separation from him felt so good. That's all I knew, until the day my mother called from the hospital. Then I had to decide: Would I see him before he died? The answer was not obvious to me. Eventually it came to feel inevitable; I had to go see him, even though I was scared. Not of his dying, but of the tension between us.

People were shocked when I stopped speaking to him. He's your father, they said. Long ago my therapist said to me in her clipped Scots accent: Miss Miller, one can either grow to accept one's parents, or, if that is not possible, one can decide not to see them. Sometimes the latter is the right choice.

I had been twenty-two then, sitting in her office in Highgate, staring at the Oriental rug, twisting a tissue. Fifteen years later I typed a note to my father. I need a respite from seeing you, it ended. He didn't reply. My mother said he was very wounded, but I believed deep down he was relieved, as tired of my condemnations as I was of his.

I first came back to Fort Lee in October. I brought Maury and the children with me because I knew he would want to see them, and also for protection. With the children there playing and needing things and Maury there to chat with him, we wouldn't have to really talk. The previous summer I had received two letters from him in quick succession. The intensity of our feelings was so high at the time that both letters were more or less histrionic, but that was the way things were for us then. The first letter, which was sent after a particularly stressful visit, was an attack. Desperate, lashing out. If you were smart, decent, good, you would realize what great parents you have. Other people love and respect me; I'm not as bad as you make me out to be. I can't bear your disdain. The rage and hurt that smoked off the page was aimed at demolishing me, sucking me in and destroying me. My hand holding the pages shook. I could hardly breathe.

The second letter arrived two days later. I love you, you are wonderful, I've been so proud of you. Letter one was unmentioned. This unnerved me. I had learned in graduate school about splitting, that the borderline personality cannot integrate good and bad, and here were the two letters, one in which I was good and one in which I was bad, and no bridge between the two. So, like Peter Rabbit caught by the buttons of his coat under the fence, I slipped out of the whole thing. I need a respite from you, I wrote, and he didn't reply.

I was very nervous about seeing him again that first time. At one point, when I went into the kitchen to get a glass of water, I turned from the sink and there he was. The kitchen was a tiny galley, barely wide enough for two people to pass. He put his hand on my arm. Susan, he said, I just want you to know— His voice caught, his eyes filled with tears. Before he could continue, I patted his shoulder. You don't have to say anything, I told him, as though I was being kind. I slipped past him, into the living room, heart pounding.

To my great relief, he didn't try to speak to me alone again that day or on the next visit, in November. During both visits I couldn't meet his eyes without looking away almost immediately, and saying almost anything to him embarrassed me.

Now I walked into his room and sat down on the folding chair that had been set up next to his bed. Weak winter sunshine, filtered by the slats of the venetian blinds, shadowed the wall above the bed with stripes of light.

He smiled gently and reached out his hand. For an instant I had no idea what he wanted. Then I leaned toward him and put my palm up to his. His fingers clasped around my hand, and my fingers answeringly closed on his. I felt through his hand his need for physical connection. I understood. It always soothed me to take Maury's hand when I was sick. I felt my father's need, so I took his hand. How could I have said no? Then I waited for the inevitable disgust to hit me, but it was as if a current had been switched off, the one that shocked me as though I had touched a fork to a toaster coil.

Nothing, there was nothing. This had never happened before. His hands had always repulsed me. They were ravaged, rotten. He did it to himself, and he kept doing it. They were always being picked at, chewed up, gnawed. He kept hurting himself. I couldn't stand it. I said to myself a million times that I was too fastidious, why should I care, they were his hands, not mine, but trying to talk myself out of my revulsion was no good. My response was visceral, uncontrollable. If I had to pick a symbol for a family crest, they would be it, his destroyed, bleeding hands.

But the disgust didn't come. I knew that when it did, I'd have to take away my hand. I wouldn't have a choice, my revulsion would be stronger than his need. But it didn't come. Its continuing absence was like a peaceful silence. I could hold his hand, just plain hold it, and nothing happened.

Always, when visiting him, I'd steel myself to glance at his hands, to check up on them, to see how they were doing, and then I'd look away and avoid them as much as possible for the rest of the visit. I'd purposely keep my eyes from resting on them. They were always a mess. Often a couple of fingers were bandaged. By the time a finger merited a bandage, it was bleeding and raw. He wrapped up the oozing finger in gauze that he covered with neatly wound strips of white surgical tape.

Tightening up my insides in preparation, I looked down now at his hands, both of which were clasped around one of mine on top of the blanket. I couldn't resist. But this time what I saw amounted to a miracle. His hands looked completely normal. He had fingernails, smooth, pinkish, nice, absolutely normal nails. Gone were the ripped skin, blank fingertips, and torn cuticles that had been chewed like food, the way a dog chews its bone. He had stopped ravaging his fingers; plainly, in the face of death, he had stopped killing himself at last.

I wouldn't have recognized his hands if they hadn't been attached to his body. Not only did these hands have nails, they were no longer the rough and calloused hands of a working man. The skin was smooth and soft. Even their shape was altered. These hands were fine, small boned, pure looking, like the hands of an angel in a medieval painting. All the pounds he had lost over the past few months may have left the rest of him cadaverous, but his hands had been reborn. They were healthy, fresh, and beautiful: a young person's hands.

Strangely, these new hands were also completely familiar. I knew I had seen them before; in fact, I knew them well. They looked just like my brother's and just like mine. My hands and Aaron's are so alike that when I'd watch Aaron roll a cigarette or open a jar, it would seem, for a disorienting, dislocating second, as if his hands were mine, as if it were me tapping the tobacco into the Zig Zag, though I'd never rolled one in my life. My mother's hands looked nothing like ours, and before today neither did my father's.

Our hands had seemed to be parentless. More or less without thinking about it, I'd check my aunts', cousins', and uncles' hands, to see if any of them were similar to ours. They weren't, nor were they as beautiful. I enjoyed watching my hands do things; sometimes I'd just look at them at school when I was bored. I wasn't vain about any part of me but my hands and my feet, and that vanity was one of aesthetic pleasure, maybe not really vanity at all. It seemed likely that two pairs of such unusual and nearly identical hands as Aaron's and mine had been directly inherited, but the donor was missing. Now I had found him.

I'm ten or fifteen or twenty, I'm sitting next to my father in the front seat of the car, and we're driving across the river to New York, or he's driving me home from a friend's house or up to college so that I don't have to take the bus and he can buy drugs, though I don't know this at the time. It is any day, alone with him in the car, and he is talking nonstop. I'm trying to listen to what he is saying, to follow along, to not get annoyed by his insistent delivery, but I can't stand it when he gets so excited about what he is saying that he begins to make the same point over and over, with his favorite phrase, "in other words," leading into another explanation of what I have already heard. I heard it and I get it, and I tell him I get it, but that doesn't stop him, which makes me angrier and angrier. He's a big force, he's hard to stop, impossible maybe.

Now he is poking my shoulder, my upper arm, with his forefinger for emphasis. I slide over closer to the door, press against it, scrunch myself up. Does he notice that I'm all the way over, all tight and pressed together, in order to get away from that finger? No, he just stretches his arm out further to get to me. I tell him again that I get it, I understand what he is trying to say. I really do get it, I'm not lying to him just so he'll shut up and put that finger down. If I didn't get it I would tell him, because I want to understand what he is saying, so that if it doesn't make sense to me, I can argue with him. Usually when I argue with him, he listens to me pretty well, much better than he listens to my scrunched-up body or my asking, Please don't poke me, neither of which penetrates through his swirling, self-centered verbosity.

He and I are what my mother calls "interested in the world." We argue about music, books, movies, not about what is going on between us, not about that poking finger, because he won't discuss that kind of thing or change it.

When he isn't talking, he is biting his nails, which are not nails. Because there is nothing really to bite on, his chewing makes a squeaking, sucking, wet noise that makes my skin crawl and my throat seize up. If both of us are quiet for a while, all you can hear is that sound. I ask him to stop, and he might for a moment, but only for a moment. He gnaws with serious concentration, working on certain bits long and hard. I ask him again to stop, but I don't scream, I just ask, pleading, Please, could you stop? It makes me furious that he would persist in something unbearable to me, that he would make me suffer just so that he can chew his fingers. The truth never occurs to me: he doesn't notice my misery.

My stiff, cold, restrained replies are designed to show him how much it costs me to put up with his habits, but his need to chew his fingers, to poke me, to repeat himself, is surpassingly greater than his need to make things even a little easier for me. He doesn't control himself, he doesn't even try, the way I am trying to not open the door, to not scream, to not hit him and kick him, to not smash his face with my fist to force him to stop.

My hand itches to open the door. I want out; the car is too small for him and me. The outside world is there, but I'm locked up in here, speeding along with him and his poking finger and his chewing and his endless talking and that noise, squeaky and wet, that goes on and on no matter what I say. I want out, but I am in for the ride. I do what I can. I picture yogis in loincloths striding over burning coals, dancing over beds of broken glass. The mind's ability to alter the body so that it will not feel pain would be a useful skill for me in many situations. I try to imagine how the yogis do it. If I concentrate hard enough, I should be able to transcend my self in the passenger seat. I try to turn my mind into a place where I can disappear. I don't want to be *not here* the way I am *not here* to my father; I want to be *not here* in a way I can will.

Listen, Susan, my father said. His voice was weak, whispery, straining to be heard. When he became really ill, the pitch of his voice began to rise. Now it seemed as if it was almost used up. He had to squeeze out his words, and some of them cracked and broke in the air. Death was trying to muzzle him, but words were everything to him; he always needed to get through, to express himself with a desperation that was maddening when you were with him and sad when you thought about it. He was going to keep death from silencing him as long as he could. It might stop him from walking, from eating, but he'd fight it tooth and nail to keep talking.

Why do you talk so much? I once asked him. He thought for a moment, then he said: You know how when you are sitting around with a bunch of people and you say something and no one answers, right away you hear the silence, and you start feeling like you said something wrong, so you try to fix it by talking some more? That's how I feel all the time, like I've said something badly or something stupid and I have to keep filling up that silence. I can't stand the silence. I hear everyone thinking, He's a shmuck.

As I sat next to him, my heart felt like a stone full of guilt.

My father's conviction that I was at fault for the troubles between us had affected me deeply, despite myself. When he experienced me as cruel, I felt cruel. I thought of the wrongly condemned—you know you are innocent, but you have been tried and found guilty, and sometimes you can't help it, this feeling of guilt comes over you, as though you had actually committed the crime. My father was not like me, susceptible to the contagion of others' opinions. Even when guilty, he experienced himself as innocent, always innocent. Those who stolidly perceive themselves as blameless are also least likely to be aware of their weaknesses, since their undergirding of self is so shaky that it cannot bear criticism. Their apparently unshakable belief in themselves is a false front; they may even know it is, but they lack the ability to strengthen what lies behind. They marshal all their energy merely to keep up the front.

After my father and I had our last huge fight, nearly two years before, my therapist asked me, Why didn't you just leave the room? My father had called me a cold bitch; he was screaming and out of control. Maury had taken the children upstairs; my mother was sitting with us in my living room, wringing her hands helplessly, a terrified expression on her face. My therapist's question stopped me cold. You could have walked out, she said. You did not have to listen to that, you did not have to be insulted. You could have said, I refuse to take part in this, we can talk about this later, when we are calmer. You could have said no.

To many, maybe even to most people, her advice would have been obvious, but to me it hadn't been. It had never crossed my mind to get up and walk out that afternoon. I had sat in the living room as though I were glued to the chair. I felt idiotic, even horrified, that it was nothing short of a revelation to me that I didn't have to stick around. What had been the matter with me that injury and insult prevailed over basic self-protection and good sense?

After that, I practiced saying no. What was I willing to accept, and at what would I draw the line? That Passover, a portion of the feminist Haggadah we used seemed to have been written for me. The Jews, freed from slavery in Egypt, were technically no longer oppressed, it said, but they had been under the thumb of the pharaoh for so long that they did not know how to be free, how to feel free. Learning to be free was a gradual and difficult process. During that seder it came to me with a pang that telling my father I needed a break from him had been only an initial step down a long, unmarked path, and that each step I took would be uncertain, stumbling, an experiment that might fail. Now, at his bedside, waiting for him to speak, I told myself, If he berates you, you can just get up and walk out the door. On the other hand, I was aware of my powerful curiosity about what he would say. This was always true for me: I was drawn to hear out the worst, the rawest vituperations from him, over which I would then stew and fume in self-righteous outrage.

I tried to ready myself for his attack. I knew that when it came, I'd have to either stay or leave, and I wasn't at all sure which choice I would make. To obscure matters further, or perhaps to clarify them, he was dying. Isn't one morally compelled, I asked myself, to listen to a dying man's words—any dying man's words—no matter what they are, insulting or not?

I waited for him to accuse me, just as I had expected his hands to repulse me, and again what I expected did not happen. This time it was my ears, not my eyes, that I could hardly believe. He was accusing himself of wrongdoing, he was shaking his head and clucking his tongue at his own misdeeds, awestruck at the extent of his failure.

He looked at me with bright, burning eyes. I was a terrible father, he said. I see that now. I acted like a fucked-up kid, running around your college buying drugs, not like a grown-up man. He was remembering, he was asking me did I remember, the night in the restaurant when he told me he had been a junkie? He was saying, When I think of the way I told you— everything I said was to make me look great. I wanted you to think I was great. I didn't think about you. I never thought of you at all as a person with feelings. I never for a moment in all your life considered how you felt.

It was the end of February. I had just turned twenty-one and had been living in Cambridge for the last two months, during my college's annual winter nonresident term, doing research on my senior thesis. I had had a difficult winter. My boyfriend had another girlfriend, who thought she was pregnant. My rented room was lonely and freezing cold; I could not use the kitchen, so I lived on apples and cheese that I kept on the windowsill. My own inadequacies glared at me. I had been too shy to ask questions of the librarians at Widener Library. Even though eventually I had gotten the information I needed, I knew I had wasted many hours trying to find it. I was writing about the poetry of Charles Olson, who had died recently. Through a friendship with a local poet, opportunities to interview friends of Olson had fallen into my lap all winter long—dinners with Robert Creeley, Elsa Dorfman, afternoons with Gordon Carney, all of them eager to talk to me and to introduce me to others. No thank you, I said. I am analyzing the texts of the poems, not writing about the man. It was a golden opportunity, but I was much too self-conscious to take it. I wouldn't be able to chat, I wouldn't be able to think of questions, I would blush and stumble and stammer and act like a jerk. I had to say no. Saying no was bad, I felt like a fool saying no, but saying yes would have been even worse. Saying yes would mean I would have to do it and I would be bad at it and then I would be mortified, and so I said, I had to say, no.

My parents drove up from New Jersey to take me home for a few days before it was time to return to Bennington for my final semester. It was evening and bitterly cold. We were on our way to dinner, and they were having a terrible argument in the front seat of the car. At a red light my mother opened the door, so angry at something I can no longer recall, that she got out by herself in the dark, icy, unfamiliar city and slammed the door. My mother was a frightened person, afraid to cross busy streets, worried about getting lost, shy about asking directions. But she was enraged, and I knew that her anger would imbue her with a bravery she did not usually possess. I watched her disappear into the night, marching off purposefully. I thought about helping her find her way back to the hotel, but I stayed in the car with my father.

We ate in the restaurant under the Orson Welles, the old art-movie house, a large, noisy, high-ceilinged room set up with long communal tables, like a medieval dining hall. It was deliciously warm inside. Smells of roasting and baking wafted out of the kitchen. In the front of the room, between the diners and the swinging doors to the kitchen, a group of musicians were setting up. Some of them were friends of mine, young jazz players who were seriously good and who came over to say hello. I was proud of my father at that moment, glad I had stayed with him, glad I let my mother go off alone, just to have that moment of watching him shake Ernie's hand, saying, How ya doing, man? I was glad to be there with the kind of father they wished they had, someone who would understand them and their music. My dad is truly hip, I said to myself. He is not some sold-out liberal, a lefty gone soft with material success, reminiscing about the old days in the Party. He is not some narrow-minded dad, loving or mean, who might as well be on another planet as far as the music goes, as far as the sensibility is concerned. My father has some faults, I told myself, but at least he is not an ordinary man.

When I was twelve, my father almost died. My mother and I and a school friend of mine were at our little lakeside cabin in upstate New York when my uncle called to say my father was in a coma at Harlem Hospital. When my mother hung up the phone, she turned to me and in a tight voice explained that my father might be dying, that she would have to leave by the next Trailways bus to Manhattan. She seemed calm and in control. She picked up the phone again and arranged for neighbors to put my friend and me on the train I had always wanted to ride, the famous Phoebe Snow, which would take us to Hoboken, where my friend's parents would pick us up.

Before my mother went out with her suitcase to stand on the side of Route 17 and wait for the bus, she told me that my father had been found unconscious in a car in Harlem in the middle of the night. The coma had been brought on by drinking, the doctors thought; alcohol was potentially lethal in combination with the diet pills that his own doctor had prescribed.

There were several puzzles for me in the story. My mother said he had gone out for a drink with some of the other window trimmers after a union meeting. But he had been found in Harlem. The District 65 building was way downtown, on

Astor Place, nowhere near Harlem. Harlem wasn't far out of his way home, but after union meetings, the men sat at one of the back tables in Ratner's and had something to eat, then drove to their houses in Long Island, Brooklyn, wherever. I couldn't imagine why they would have gone all the way up to Harlem. And Harlem simply wasn't a place where the all-white constituency of the window trimmers hung out. I knew my father had some jobs trimming windows in women's shops on Lenox Avenue, but I had never heard him say a word about socializing there. He used to go to Harlem to hear jazz, but that was before Birdland and other clubs opened up in midtown.

There was another thing I couldn't figure out. If alcohol and diet pills were a lethal combination, his doctor must have warned him not to drink. We kept a bottle of Smirnoff vodka in the kitchen cabinet, and sometimes if there was company my parents might add a bottle of gin, but when the company left, the bottles gathered dust. My mother never drank hard liquor and my father scarcely did, and then never alone. Sometimes, on a hot day, he'd have a beer. I thought of both my parents as abstemious, but this was normal; none of my relatives drank. When I was in college, I was shocked to discover that people actually sat around at home having drinks, just like in the movies. So it made no sense to me that my father would knowingly (for it seemed certain that the doctor would have warned him) risk his life for a drink.

While my mother was packing and making arrangements, I went out alone in the rowboat, far enough from shore that the cottage looked small. Bungalows dotted the shoreline all around: little mildewy unheated summer houses like ours, sited depressingly on bare dirt, since no grass could grow under the oppressive pines. I found the dankness of the house claustrophobic, and much preferred the open water. Sometimes I'd row slowly halfway around the lake to the water lilies; sometimes I'd pretend I had a vital message that had to get to the other side and I'd pull hard and fast straight across. This time I just rowed out a ways and then drifted, letting myself experience in privacy the thrill of imagining my father dead. Minutes after my mother hung up the heavy black receiver and turned to me to say he might die, it struck me like a thunderbolt that if he did, it would be a great relief. If he died, our problems would be solved.

I didn't understand why I felt this way. After all, he wasn't home very often, so losing him for good wouldn't on the face of it change things that much. Yet I knew that his death would be the answer, that we would be much better off without him.

Sitting across the table from my father in the Orson Welles, eating roast chicken, I was still as ignorant of what had really happened that night in Harlem as I had been when I was twelve.

The conversation turned to musician friends of his who had been junkies. I had known for some time that some of the musicians had been addicts; he had talked before about friends being busted, sent to jail. Cabaret cards were taken away in those days if you got caught. You had to have a cabaret card to play in a club in New York, and if you couldn't play in New York, you had no life. Drug laws were very harsh; there was mandatory sentencing if you were caught with heroin. Some of the musicians survived the police harassment, jail, and suspension of their cards and went on to become famous, like Stan Getz, and others died of overdoses. Others, even though they had great talent, survived but drifted into obscurity. One of them was my father's good friend the vocalist David Allen, who, with a drug habit in his prime and without a cabaret card, lost his chance at fame.

My father was talking while eating his chicken quickly, with his fingers. He always ate fast and always talked at the same time. He said, Heroin is not bad for you physically. It's not the heroin that kills you. In fact, I once read that it's a kind of preservative. What's dangerous is the way you have to live to get it. That's why you don't see too many elderly junkies. In the end you either overdose and die or else you get to the point in your life where you just can't make the scene anymore. You just get too old to be going where you have to go and doing what you have to do to get the stuff. You just can't make it anymore, so you quit. That's what happened to me.

I didn't stop him. I didn't yell out, What are you telling me? I just listened and finished my dinner, and all the time I had this funny, cold feeling. I got back to my room and I called up my old friend Lynn and I said, Guess what, I think my father just told me he used to be a heroin addict. And as I said it, I knew it was the truth.

I got in the car with my parents the next morning to drive to Fort Lee. I wanted to know everything, but I was afraid. However, the subject never came up. My mother just talked and sang along to the radio in her off-key voice. My father talked a lot, as usual. It was pouring rain, and we all made funny comments when we passed a car that was also a boat. Two, three hours passed. Why wasn't anyone bringing this up? Hadn't my father told my mother what he had said to me? Did he think I hadn't understood him? After all, he had told me in a very offhand manner, and I hadn't responded. Maybe he told me unconsciously, unaware he had done so. What was the truth? I had a million questions, but the crucial one—had he really been a junkie?—sat like an unexploded bomb in my hands. I dared not pull the pin there, with all of us enclosed for hours in the car.

My father squeezed my hand between both of his and gave it a little affirmative shake. I just want you to know that I know that you've never done anything bad to me, he said.

Thank you, I replied. I knew it, but it's good to hear you say so.

I hardly knew what I was saying, and, by this time, I was crying too hard to say more, a flood of silent, unquenchable tears running down my cheeks and dropping onto my shirt. I took a tissue and mopped my face, but the tears welled up again and again, sobless, refilling my eyes as they overflowed.

His words evaporated what felt like a physical weight on my shoulders. There was a stillness in me, as though all the molecules of my being had stopped an angry, anxious dance. Often I had felt how anger makes things jump around, become restless in themselves, go crazy. Suddenly all was calm. The lamp, the books on the shelves, the ugly vinyl reclining chair with its head back and its footrest up, had become simplified, more solid. The million molecules that made up the bedroom were at rest in their objects—shoe, desk, wristwatch—peaceful and still.

Pulling tissue after tissue out of the box on the little bedside table, I was awash in tears and gratitude and sadness. He was saying everything I had ever wanted him to say.

Suddenly, I laughed a harsh, bitter laugh.

It's so ironic, I heard myself saying, not knowing what I meant.

Yes, it is, he said sympathetically, as though he understood.

With what was he agreeing? My mind scrambled for the irony that some part of me had detected, the source of that bitter laugh. Perhaps it lay in his saying all these wonderful things at the last possible moment, which this was and which, in any event, nothing could have guaranteed. It was true that a snowstorm, a child's fever, or any one of the million accidents of life could have kept me away from his bedside. Then there was death. For all he knew, he could have died suddenly last night, and then the words that to any ears but mine would have sounded so terrible—I never for a moment thought about how you felt—would never have been said. They were the best, most comforting words I had ever heard. I knew that the rest of my life would be different because I had heard them. By waiting so long, he had taken the chance I never would.

These words came from outside the layers of self-referential fog through which he saw me refracted, a blurry shape with certain enumerable traits. He longed for my approval—really, my adoration. I had been almost a figment of his imagination; I had never, essentially, taken on for him a separate corporeal reality.

That was how it was. I had always known it but didn't believe it. Was it possible, I'd ask myself, that a human being who was as intelligent, as full of ideas and perceptions as he was, could also be nearly sightless? No, it wasn't possible; he must, I'd tell myself, perceive me, even empathize with me, more than I know. I would try to pick up those vibrations, but none came through.

Now at last some did; the change was perceptible to me, in me. He had not completely transformed or he would not have played this game with chance. He would have told me sooner; he would have known its importance. He was still the center of his own world; that much had not changed. He had for the first time succeeded at being a father by telling me he had failed as a father. That was good and that was true, but why had he waited so impossibly long?

Waiting like this had assured him of no consequences, no stumbling and failing in a new role, no awkward trying to be the father he now realized he had never been. Death had given him the mental room, the safety and security, to face and speak his failure.

Five years before, I told him over the phone that I had been doing a lot of thinking about how Aaron used to beat me up. My father said, Beat you up? I don't know what you're talking about.

I had been standing at my kitchen sink, doing the dishes, the receiver tucked between my chin and shoulder. Eleanor, who was a baby, was asleep upstairs. Our house, which initially had seemed to me, after a lifetime in apartments, to be eerily quiet and large, now sheltered and rooted me. Since birth I had moved every two or three years; already Maury and I had been in our house longer than that and had no intention of leaving. It had been built as a worker's home in the late 1800s: nine small-ish rooms on three floors. There was no wasted space, only one bathroom and a few small closets, but it had a nice, private yard, old lilacs and apple trees, and a simple charm. I had learned the names of flowers as I planted a garden of scabiosa, cornflowers, flax, daisies, and basket-of-gold.

The kitchen was old and decaying, the mottled linoleum so ancient it crumbled under our feet. There was an old hulking stove and not one drawer or countertop. The kitchen windows looked out on the yard, except for one that faced the blank siding of the house next door. It was through this window that I looked as I gathered up courage to say to my father that I had been thinking about me and Aaron. I was mentioning the unmentionable, breaking the taboo that had stopped any of us from talking about Aaron's punches and kicks and why they were not restrained and what they did to me and what they did to him. Or at least until that moment I believed it was a taboo, not my parents' ignorance, that silenced us.

My father's response stunned me. You know, I insisted, how he used to hit me, how he beat me up all the time, every day.

My father said, If anything like that happened, I didn't know about it.

Come on, I said, not believing my ears, it happened all the time. It was a big problem. Once you hit him for it, you lost control. You beat him up yourself, it was really horrible. Don't you remember that?

It had been in the early days of the diet pills, when we lived in Fort Lee, on Federspiel Street. I had come into the living room, crying, because Aaron had hurt me. I was about ten. I didn't often appeal for help, and I cannot recall why I did that day, but I do remember that my father, to my great surprise, jumped up, rushed into my brother's room, grabbed him and started beating him, which he had never done before. I was amazed. This, I thought, was going to be the end of Aaron hitting me. My father was going to stop him. Finally someone was protecting me. But my father could not stop hitting Aaron. My mother threw herself on him, trying in vain to drag his frenzied bulk off my brother, who was cowering and sobbing, covering his head with his hands to ward off my father's blows. My mother screamed at my father to stop—he was going to kill Aaron. She pulled at my father's T-shirt, but it just stretched in her hand. Later, when it was over, my mother blamed the diet pills. They get him all wound up, she explained.

Since it was not repeated, I assumed my father must have been as terrified of his rage as we were. That he never interceded on my behalf again I took to mean that he could not trust himself to do so. He might indeed kill Aaron to protect me, and he couldn't risk that.

On the phone my father repeated, impatiently, I don't know anything about it. He sounded bored and irritable. He didn't ask me to tell him what happened, what it was he didn't know.

As a child I didn't feel love for my father. Perhaps I didn't let myself feel it, but I knew I didn't. Books, movies, television, other children, teachers, other adults told me that children love their parents. It was the 1950s, and that was all you heard. *I Remember Mama*, *Ozzie and Harriet*, *Father Knows Best*. I tried as hard as I could to find love in myself for him. I searched for it in every nook and cranny of my being. I held up to the light the feelings I had about him, and I turned them this way and that, wondering if another person might see love in them. I kept thinking, Love must be here, somewhere. I looked and looked inside myself, but I couldn't find it.

I knew what love was. It was the feeling I had for my dolls, for beautiful things, for certain friends. Later on, when I knew Debbie, my best friend, I felt even more sure that love was what made you feel good. Love was not what made you feel bad, hate yourself. It was what comforted you, freed you up inside, made you laugh. Sometimes Debbie and I would fight, but that was different, because we were basically, essentially connected.

I hadn't been sure if I loved my mother and my brother, but they were real to me in ways my father wasn't. Why should I have loved him? He never noticed anything that happened to me. But Aaron beating me, I was sure he knew about that. It had been, after all, the most prominent, consistent feature of my childhood. Now, hanging up the phone, I shivered and my hands shook. He knew nothing. He had been more blind than I had imagined. Monstrously blind. Worse yet, he still didn't want to know anything, like the good Germans who claimed they did not know, did not see, and still could not believe. We all say it was impossible for them not to have known, what with the stench and the freight cars going in full and coming out empty. These Germans didn't want to know because if they had known, they would also have known that they were not doing anything to stop what was going on behind the barbed wire, and that they were not doing anything to stop it because they were not outraged.

Of course, I knew there was no comparison between the Germans and a boy who needed to be stopped from beating, smothering, arm twisting. But the denial was the same. You bruise so easily, my mother would say, looking with her perpetually heartbroken eyes at my perpetually black-and-blue arms and legs, convinced that the blotches were caused by my clumsily bumping into the coffee table or the corner of an open drawer. My father never commented on my bruises at all.

I knew that this beating was so much a part of our family's daily routine that it was hardly noticed. It was accepted as Aaron's need, just as my mother expected him to get hungry at lunchtime and want to eat. This need to strike out came from an accretion of anger. That was how I understood it. It was necessary for him to express his anger every few hours or so, when it got to be of a certain urgency. Once vented on me, his hostility began to collect again, drip by drip. Just as no one expects hunger to be satisfied once and for all, so no one expected him to cure his anger this way, but just to scratch its itch on me.

My mother used to plead with him to stop. I took this to mean that it was right for me not to like being hit. But, then, in a tête-à-tête with me, she said, How could he help it? He had been treated so badly by her as an infant. This rage of his was legitimate in her eyes, and it rubbed salt into the wound of her guilt over an old crime against him that even to my naive, childish mind did not seem heinous enough to justify such anger so many years after the fact. The crime had been not feeding him enough when he was an infant, she said, because she had stuck to the rigid bottle-feeding schedule rec-ommended at that time. Baby Aaron had cried constantly. He was starving, she said. I let him starve.

Finally she had given him more bottles and he quieted. He was six months old. The doctor told her all along that he was not underweight, but she said she knew he needed more food, and she could not forgive herself for not giving it to him.

I heard this story for the first time when I was seven or eight. It made me queasy. The storm of violent emotions in it, and her adamancy, scared me. Also, the equation she had set up was not a balanced one. How could not feeding him enough for a few months result in his complex, opaque anger so many years later? I didn't think this in words, through logic. I felt: something is wrong here, do not believe this, these reasons are not completely right.

My mother talked as if Aaron's anger was incurable, as if nothing could be done to change it. If that were true, I would have to be beaten forever and my mother would always be in pain. I could not accept this. I wanted her to feel better, and I would have tried anything to pull her up from the despair that weighed her down. The worse Aaron behaved, the greater was her guilt, and the deeper she sank. She was wrong, she had to be wrong, and I would work hard to convince her she was.

I put the phone receiver back in its cradle, and I stood in the kitchen, staring at the chalky white siding of the house next door. The dishes sat half done in the sink. At least my mother had felt guilty; she had pitied me. She did nothing, but she felt for me. My brother hurt me, but in some way he, too, had pitied me, as I also pitied him. But what had my father felt? Now I knew: he had felt nothing at all, because he knew nothing. A complete and perfect defense.

Susan, my father rasped. He pulled tighter on my hand, drawing me nearer to him and to the words that faltered and came so hard. Susan, you see, I didn't know anything about a family. Nothing. Not how to be in one, not how to make one, not even how to imagine one. I had no example. You know, I never heard my father once call my mother by her first name. "Mrs. Miller," he always called her, and with such hate.

This came as no surprise to me. As a child I had been convinced that if my father saw me in an unexpected place, away from the clues that linked me to him, such as my mother or my school, he would not recognize me. Having no knowledge of drugs, I could not say to myself, He is stoned, he is high. But even if he had not been an addict, he would not have been a good father. I knew this because my mother had told me so: my father had come to parenthood ignorant of love, acquainted only with hate.

My parents would wryly imitate my grandfather calling his wife either Mrs. Miller, as though in quotes, or Sweetyhearts, with sarcastic venom and in a Yiddish accent: Sveetyhearts. I was familiar with the hate in the house on Brighton Third Street, where my father grew up, because I had heard about it for as long as I could remember, both as a tragedy and, because it had been so excessive, as a comedy, as overdone, as close to ridiculous.

It was mostly my mother who talked to me seriously about my father's family. And I saw things for myself. As I grew older, I observed that in their relationships with each other—but, more horrifying, in their relationships with everyone—hate was accepted at face value but kindness was suspected of being manipulation, a cover to gain a desired and selfish end.

My mother told me that when my father first met her mother, Surah Berman, he simply did not believe that she could be as nice as she seemed. He pushed and prodded her over months but she remained warm to him, gentle and generous. Eventually he came to the conclusion that what he saw in his mother-in-law had to be genuine, that there was no nasty "real" person lurking underneath. My father spoke of her kindness in tones that still conveyed amazement long after she was dead. In knowing her, he had beheld one of the wonders of the world: a thoroughly nice person. His conviction that she was genuinely good did not generalize, however. She was an anomaly.

In the same vein, his view of social niceties was that they merely papered over, as he was fond of saying, "man's inhumanity to man." As I grew up, I came more and more to realize that my father had a sense of the monstrous not only in himself but in all of us.

My mother told me stories when I was growing up about my grandmother Esther, the wicked witch of Brighton Beach. According to my mother, my grandmother despised men. She lavished attention on her daughter, Sarah, my father's only sibling. Esther dealt in machinations, lies, and deceptions, feeding the fires of hatred between father and son, sister and brother, so that for weeks this one wouldn't speak to that one, that one wouldn't speak to this one, everyone crushed together in the one basement room where they lived. When my father did well in school, his mother scorned him. She tore up a citation he'd won—and then spat on it. She never kissed him, except on the day he went off to boot camp. His mother and my mother, then his young wife, were standing on the platform, saying goodbye. Seeing the other mothers tearfully embracing their sons, Esther was shamed into touching hers: she pecked his cheek.

My mother let me know there were other tales of Esther as a parent that were too terrible for me to hear, being only a child. She said she was telling me these things so that I would understand why my father was difficult, why he had, as she put it, "trouble with love." I felt sorry for him—and who would not, hearing that he grew up in a kind of loveless hell?

When my father spoke of his childhood, he rarely mentioned the dreadful life inside the house. He talked of his not-dreadful life outside, on the streets, the beach, the boardwalk, the handball courts, and in the candy stores, the Ping-Pong and pool halls. What had gone on in his house was terrible, he let us know that, but he didn't tell us much. When I was older, I asked him questions about his parents. What towns were they originally from? What was his mother's maiden name? What was his father's last name, before it was changed at Ellis Island? He didn't know the answers to any of these questions; his parents never spoke about their childhoods in Poland. He said that he was sure they had had awful lives there, literally unspeakable, although the details were completely unknown to him. He said they never spoke about their early lives because they wanted to forget them. By dumping their pasts overboard on the crossing, they could set new feet on the New World shores.

When it came time for my father to cross over to parenthood from childhood, he too came with his lips sealed. He couldn't stop talking, but not about what had happened in the house on Brighton Third. My grandmother had many framed family photographs on the walls of her apartment; my mother pointed out to me that not one of them was of Sidney, not even of Sidney as a baby, or of me or Aaron. They were all of Sarah, my father's sister, and her husband and son and daughter. My mother railed about this injustice, this pointed cruelty; my father responded to her with only slow, sad shakes of his head and resigned, philosophical shrugs that signaled to me a pain too great to reduce to words.

My mother said that Esther hated men. It didn't matter who they were, what they did; she hated them all. My grandmother saw the relations between women and men as a battle you fought by any means necessary. Lying, withholding sexual favors, granting those favors, provoking jealousy were the well-used weapons in her arsenal. Just as she shunned my father, she doted on her daughter and trained her carefully. Sarah boasted to my mother that she could get her husband to do what she wanted by refusing to sleep with him; it never fails, she said, though sometimes it takes several weeks.

They had this discussion in my aunt's bedroom, where she had taken my mother to show her a new fur coat. Her husband, the manager of an A&P, could not afford the fancy dresses and shoes that were stuffed into my aunt's closet, but each visit, newly acquired items were brought out for display. You could have such treasures, too, Sarah advised my mother, if you just played your cards right.

I would never do that to your father. I could never use him like that, no matter what it was I wanted, my mother said, relating the story to me later. I was about twelve or thirteen at the time. In Sarah's opinion, my mother was a dowdy fool, too stupid to make proper use of her marriage.

My mother wanted me to understand my father, or at least have sympathy for him. She also wanted to express her own outrage and hurt at the way she was treated by Esther and Sarah. Esther's idea of beauty was the bleached-blond bombshell, not my shy, plain, spectacled, minimally made-up mother. I was my mother's "only friend," she said, and she had to talk to someone. I felt sorry for my father, I was wary of my grandmother, and I learned to listen. I received and felt my mother's pain. I learned that there were terrible people in the world and that my grandmother was one of them. I learned that there were victims in the world, and my father was one of them.

When my brother was little, Esther presented him with gifts that were wildly inappropriate in size, like tiny infant booties when he was three or four years old. My mother was sure that my grandmother did not have a perceptual problem and that these gifts were deliberate insults, though their meaning was opaque. Later my grandmother took to handing out quarters to Aaron and me when we came to visit. She spoke to us harshly in Yiddish, which we did not understand, and roughly pressed the coins into our palms.

According to my mother, the only way in which Esther had expressed affection to her son had been by serving him huge quantities of food, which laid the foundation for my father's compulsive eating. He stripped the refrigerator of food during the night, so that in the morning whatever we had hoped to bring to school for lunch was gone, along with nearly everything else. He gobbled his food, his head close to his plate. He ate all the time. He ate while reading, while watching TV. He ate bunches of grapes, bags of oranges, bowls of cottage cheese, the foods of dieters, but in enormous quantities.

On Sunday evenings we frequently went to Chinatown for dinner with my Aunt Sarah and her family. Our usual restaurant was Wo Kee, in a basement on Pell Street, located down steep, sour-smelling steps. The windowless dining room was full of clatter and crash and delicious smells from the food, which at first had frightened me with its long noodles like worms and thick lumpy sauces, but which I finally tried and loved. The eight of us would sit at a long table, passing tea and dishes, my aunt and my father loudly arguing, not over things personal but over politics or the meaning of a book. The food disappeared quickly, so if I wanted more, I had to hurry. My mother chewed methodically, sitting prim and straight, speaking in a low voice, cautioning me to eat slowly, chew my food well. But the food was escaping from me, my father and my aunt grabbing at it, sucking on lobster claws, downing in two gulps whole egg rolls dripping with duck sauce and hot mustard, raving about the food as they attacked it, pronouncing it good, great, the best yet, scraping out the last drops of sauce from the footed metal dishes. My father and my aunt were large and loud and animated, the rest of us a sort of audience for them, picking at their leavings and scarcely noticed. We were like chickens scurrying off the tracks because here comes the big locomotive, and it won't stop for us. Brother and sister ran the meal, and it was against them that we competed for food and for air in the close, steamy room.

Good as her food might have been, eating with Esther could not have been an unmitigated pleasure. How was cute, smart little Sidney to know if what was piled on his plate was love or not love—not, in fact, a sort of hate, or hate mixed with love, like the witch stuffing Hansel full so she could devour him? A kind of control through enjoyment, through being forced to eat and to keep eating out of fear that rejection of the food would be unbearable to the server. Therefore, the boy must eat until the server is full. If he doesn't, the server will respond with rage instead of with the praise the boy wants, the only praise he gets. So, the story goes, Esther fed Sidney fuller than full, so that he got heavier and heavier, used to quantities larger than he needed but never large enough for her, and then, finally, never large enough for him either.

In those days he was athletic—swimming, running on the boardwalk and the beach—so that he was heavy but not really fat. When Sarah had a son, she stuffed him until he was obese, shocking to look at in the brown-tinted photos that show him standing on his front steps at age eight, nine, ten. He is tethered there by his weight. He looks unable to move, imprisoned in his body's cage—though his clever mind, through which he later earned escape, I must assume was ticking away.

My father sometimes reminisced about his mother's fabulous kishka and stuffed derma. Her pastry was so legendary that one day a neighborhood teenager crept through the open basement window and made off with an entire, uncut, cooling strudel. My father always laughed, telling how his mother ran into the street, outraged, screaming, Gonif! Gonif! (Thief! Thief!) at the top of her voice, a short, stocky bundle of fury.

I loved this story, how the thief got to eat the whole, delicious pastry all by himself, away from my awful grandmother, out of range of her eyes and voice. I loved the image of my grandmother rushing out into the street in her housedress, shouting, unself-conscious, a funny figure, but there was bravery in this—to shout at the top of your lungs for what was yours, to want to kill for it, to not know decorum. It was deliciously satisfying that my grandmother had been driven wild, for once the tormented, not the tormentor. And, perhaps best of all, this was a story of liberation, about a strudel freed from its intended fate as one of her precious, carefully crafted temptations.

My Aunt Sarah and Uncle Jack live on the fifth floor of a brand-new redbrick apartment complex, near the water in Brighton Beach but far from the shops and hustle and bustle of Brighton Beach Avenue. Their building is one of four set together in a group. The buildings are tall, seven stories, and they are all exactly the same, flat and narrow, like cornflake boxes with windows cut out. My aunt paints bright watercolors of vases of flowers, trees blowing in the wind, the ocean and bobbing boats, and her pictures are hung up in the living room, which is also where the dining table is. Last year, when she saw me in my first pair of glasses, she said that she was glad she was nearsighted because everything looks to her like an Impressionist painting.

Sarah, though I don't know it until I am in my thirties, is addicted to Benzedrine. She has a lot of energy and talks and talks. Uncle Jack is quiet and bland, but his job impresses me. I don't know anyone else who runs anything as important and complicated as an A&P. Their son, Robert, who was very fat when he was little, is off at Cornell University; my parents say that means he is exceptionally smart. My cousin Carol is thirteen, three years older than I am. They used to live in an old house in Brighton Beach, but a few years ago they moved here, which they are happy about, because the building is new and their apartment has a view.

I have never spent the night here before. My cousin Carol and I don't really get along. Her skin is thick, almost rubbery, and her eyes are narrow, like Japanese or Chinese eyes, and her nose is flat. She's not pretty at all, but she's not ugly either. She wears tight slacks and tight blouses, and lipstick, and hairspray on her teased hair. When Aaron is around, she teases or ignores me. They whisper and point at me and laugh, or they walk off together and close the door and won't let me in. Last time we visited, the three of us were down at the beach near her house; all of a sudden they ran away into the bushes and I called to them but they were gone. I had to find my way back by myself, and when I did, they were playing gin rummy on the coffee table and I could tell from Carol's face that she hoped they had scared me. I know it was Carol's idea to leave me; Aaron goes along because Carol is older and she touches his arm and looks into his eyes. Otherwise, he wouldn't leave me alone like that in case I got lost. He doesn't really want that to happen to me. She gets him to plot ways to humiliate me, and then they both laugh at my misery, but I know that, deep down, he feels bad.

Today, however, she wants to talk to me. She takes me into her bedroom, and she does that thing to me that she does to Aaron. She shuts the door, and we sit down on the floor and lean our backs against the railing of her bed. She looks me right in the eye as if she really likes me a lot, as if she wants to impress me, and she starts to talk proudly about how a boy she likes felt her up and French-kissed her behind a bush in the park; she says words like *hard-on*, which give me butterflies in my stomach. She's confiding in me, even though I'm so much younger; she's telling me secret stuff, things that she says not to repeat to anyone, especially my mother and father, but she says she knows she can trust me. It is flattering, getting attention from her, the way her eyes are focused on me, searching my face. I wonder if it's all true. Does she really put her tongue in boys' mouths and let them put their hands down her blouse? Big dicks, tits—I'm sick to my stomach but I half suspect she is saying all this just to make me squirm, so I keep nodding attentively, as if I'm at my music lesson and the teacher is explaining the scales.

My parents said they would pick me up at lunchtime, but it's lunchtime now and they are not here. They don't come and they don't come and I am missing them terribly. We have lunch without them, but I am so nervous I can hardly eat. I am trapped and panicky, using all my energy to rein in my terror that I have been forgotten, that I will be left here among these unsafe people forever. When it is time for dessert, my aunt brings out bowls of fresh strawberries and heavy cream. I have never had fresh strawberries before; my mother buys only frozen strawberries, which come sliced in syrupy juice. Eat, Sarah commands me. They're good, you will like them. Eat. I bite into one, but the fleshy texture revolts me. I can't make the berry go down. Her voice gets loud and angry. If you don't eat them, I'll stuff them down your throat, she says. I fill my spoon with cream and a small piece of berry and gulp it down whole, as if it is a pill. I eat the whole bowlful this way, not chewing, not tasting, just gagging and swallowing chunks down. She stands watching me. Good girl, she says when I am finished. Then the doorbell rings; it is my mother and I run to her, my savior.

Your father is unable to truly love, my mother would tell me, though if he loves anyone, he loves you.

Esther came to the United States in steerage when she was sixteen, from somewhere in Poland. I was told she came alone, that she had no family or friends with her and no one to meet her on the other side. My father never knew her maiden name or the name of her shtetl. Whatever relatives she left behind would have been wiped out by Hitler, so that even if I had names of places, they would lead me only to ovens long cold or ditches full of bodies long rotted.

Esther told no tales. What exactly was it she wanted to forget? Poverty, ignorance, and pogroms like so many other immigrants, but in her case I also have to imagine abuse and cruelty. As a young girl she would have had to drink a foul potion day after day to become the woman my mother called a witch.

How did she feel, I sometimes wondered, when the Nazis destroyed everything and everyone she had left behind so many years before? Could it have been a ghastly wish fulfillment, making that which she wanted to forget literally disappear?

Esther met my grandfather Max Miller on the boat coming over. He was a few years older and also alone. They clung to each other in the misery of steerage and then in the huge, strange city. They married out of fear, out of the need to have someone. They had two children, Sarah first, then Sidney. They lived uptown, in Harlem, while Max worked in the garment district and Esther saved money until they had enough to leave Manhattan, to move out to Coney Island. There Esther opened up a grocery store. Even though she was illiterate, both in Yiddish and in English, she made money. When their apartment burned down in a great fire that destroyed much of Coney

Island, they relocated up the boardwalk to Brighton Beach, a community of Yiddish-speaking refugees from the slums of Manhattan who lived in small, closely packed houses on numbered streets. The El ran along and darkened Brighton Beach Avenue, the noisy, busy shopping street where the numbered side streets ended; beyond it was the wide boardwalk, the even wider beach, and the big, changing sea.

Esther scrimped, saved, worked, and finally bought a plain-faced, stuccoed three-story house, where she would live until her death. The family moved into the basement and rented out the other units. Their basement apartment was essentially one room, a big space where beds, tables, and chairs were arranged. My mother told me that the first time she visited there, as my father's fiancée, she had been touched by the private world my father had created for himself by stacking scavenged milk crates into a partition around his bed. There he kept his books and records in neat and careful order.

We visited my grandparents in that basement, for my grandmother did not move upstairs into the first-floor apartment until my grandfather died, when I was seven. I remember the basement only as dark and gloomy, with my grandfather sitting at the table with a closed face, playing endless games of solitaire, not saying a word. My mother tells me now that he spoke English fairly well, but I don't remember him speaking to me or touching me. I recall him only at a distance, myself in the doorway, him at the table, dealing out the game. I have no memory of how his skin or clothes felt or how he smelled. In contrast, my mother's father, who died when I was four, had a mustache so bristly it scraped. He smelled clean and fresh, even though he was old and sick. His eyes smiled at me and I leaned comfortably against his thin, welcoming chest. My father's father lived three years longer, and I saw him often, but my recollection of him is nearly blank. Did he ever kiss me, hug me, talk to me? I just do not know.

My father only once told me a story about himself and his mother. I was a college student at the time. The two of us were driving on the highway on a beautiful, clear, cold winter day. My father was behind the wheel. Fourteen years earlier, in 1956, when he was thirty-eight, his father, who had been very sick, died in the hospital while my father and Esther were visiting him. My father took Esther home to Brooklyn, where she asked him for a favor. There were some terms in her will she wanted to review, but, being illiterate, she needed help. Would he read the will out loud to her? My father was tired and upset and somewhat puzzled that his mother wished to go over her will on the night of her husband's death, but he agreed. As my father talked, I pictured Esther unlocking the black metal strongbox with the key she wore around her neck and handing him the will. They would have been sitting on her overstuffed flowered chairs, knees almost touching, her heavy-featured face impassive, his eyes wary but hoping to please.

The will turned out to be simple: Esther's house and savings were to go to Sarah, her daughter. Then he heard himself, the fly in the web, reading: And to my son, Sidney, I leave nothing, because he is no good.

My father stared at the road ahead.

Why, I cried, would she have you read that to her? What did you do?

My father's voice was tired and bitter. She wanted to see what I would do, he said. She wanted to watch my reaction. Ma, I said, I gotta go home now. I'm tired and it's late. I didn't want to show her how bad I felt. I didn't want to give her the satisfaction. It wasn't the money. I didn't care about that. Let my fucking sister have the money. But why did she have to write that sentence? Why did she have me read it?

My father started to cry. He had never cried in front of me. His hands loosened their grip on the wheel. The car began to drift into the opposite lane, across the white, unbroken line.

Look out! I yelled. He grabbed the wheel and turned us toward safety. Look out, I had yelled, and he did. Look out, I had yelled, for what else could I have said?

The stucco house was not a place to learn about love. I knew that, because in that house no love was given to me. I meant as little to them as a stick of wood lying on the street. That was how it felt.

Shortly after my grandfather died, my grandmother moved upstairs into a real apartment, with a kitchen I never saw her cook in, a living room with a television and a telephone, and a tiny bedroom that used to be a porch. It is after Max's death that Esther comes into focus for me, though not as a person usually does, because we could not talk to each other, I not speaking any Yiddish and she not speaking any English. I got to know her just from being near her, from her feel, force, and skin, as you get to know creatures that do not speak, or the way you get to know storm or sunshine. It affects you, it's there, but you can't talk to it.

My grandmother was short and her legs were bowed. Her hips and shoulders were broad, her tush and bosom flat, or at least drooped. She gave an impression of strength. Her arms looked powerful. Her legs and arms were hairless and her skin was very white. It had a firm, spongy quality that fascinated and repelled me. Her body and her apartment smelled peculiar, sweet, not like applied perfume but like a scent excreted right from her tight pores.

On her broad face ("coarse," my mother called it) she wore, even to the beach, a thick layer of dead-white powder. Each of her cheeks bore a circle of bright-red rouge. Her hair was so thin you could see her waxen scalp and the dark roots of each strand, dyed a shade that was meant to be auburn but was actually bright, rusty orange. At home she wore flowered house-dresses and scuffs and usually a pair of stockings rolled down around her ankles. On the beach I would observe her twisted, gnarled toes, horned and lumpy with bunions. My grand-mother looked weird, very weird, but her house was always neat, her clothes were clean; she took care of herself. My parents were always saying she was crazy, but they meant crazy, not *crazy*, because she wasn't crazy as if her life were falling apart. Not at all.

My grandmother's kitchen table was covered in oilcloth, which reminded me of the texture of her skin and was perme-ated with that mysterious, cloying smell of hers. I heard about her wonderful cooking, but that was all in the past. She never, as far as I remember, prepared anything for us to eat on our Sunday visits to her house. I have only one memory of her serv-ing me food. It was a dish of cottage cheese, and I sat to eat it at the table. When she put it in front of me, I didn't want it, because the smell of the oilcloth, which was the smell of her skin, was too strong around it. It was as if the thick, cakey pow-der on her face had sifted down into the white curds. I knew this wasn't true, I knew it was just cottage cheese from the store that she was serving me, but I still couldn't eat it.

My grandmother's bedroom was the enclosed porch;

between it and the living room was a window that could still be raised or lowered. The bedroom was so small that there was room only for her bed and a dresser. Arranged on top of her dresser and arrayed against the quilted satin bedspread were her dolls, whose heads, arms, and torsos were made of lightweight, brittle, hollow celluloid. They each had pretty rosebud lips and crimped, wavy "real" hair, but it was their dresses, not their faces, that were on display. Huge, billowy, many-layered skirts of stiff papery fiber—the top and bottom layers dusty white, with pink, blue, and yellow sandwiched between—functioned as stands for the legless dolls.

The way my grandmother packed these dolls into her tiny room, so that every surface was covered with them, and the way they were so carefully arranged, told me she loved them. The rule was that I could look at them but I could not play with them, which I didn't mind because these dolls did not entice me as dolls usually did. I didn't feel them to be dolls at all but something else altogether, something I didn't understand.

Dolls were to be moved, to be given voices and names and characters, but these dolls stared at me with cold, dead eyes. They didn't want to play. I knew that these dolls held some key to my grandmother, like the endless tablecloths she embroidered in the screamingly loudest colors she could find, each stitch a different hue. I knew that her eyes must see differently from mine, because my ugly seemed to be her beautiful, and her dolls made my chest ache with sadness, part of which came from the dolls' disconcerting illusion of legs. You could tell they didn't have legs only if you picked them up. A doll had to have all her parts, just like a person. If she didn't, she was a crippled doll, which was all right, which was something to act out. But these dolls clearly weren't cripples. You were supposed to think they were whole, that they had legs. That they didn't wasn't supposed to matter.

My grandmother did not wield her past to inflict torment on her family. She did not accuse: How could you do this or that to me when you know what I've been through? Her story was not used as a tool, but the effects of it were rampant. She was a carrier of suffering, ignorance, and rage; that was what her whole being spoke of. She was at one with her past: it was not a story to be told, analyzed, bemoaned. It was simply lived.

We sometimes took my grandmother to Ratner's for dinner. Ratner's was a kosher dairy restaurant on lower Second Avenue, where, twenty-four hours a day, an aged waiter with a heavy Yiddish accent brought you baked fish or kasha *varniskes* or blintzes or icy *shav*. Later, when the neighborhood became the East Village, I would occasionally return to Ratner's for a plate of blintzes, after seeing the Grateful Dead at the Fillmore East next door. But at the time I was ten, eleven, twelve, and I was trying to learn the rules of public behavior. My grandmother, the urban peasant, did not give a shit about public behavior. The peasant: belching, slurping, sucking the fish bones. Picking her teeth with the corner of a matchbook. Unbuttoning her blouse to adjust her straps. It was amazing to watch her, truly not giving a damn about anyone or anything except the food in front of her.

When Esther belched, my mother said nothing. The daughter of immigrants herself, she was shy and scared inside, always afraid to make a fuss. But I was ashamed, sitting there in silence, eating my baked fish and looking up at the huge, ugly oil portrait of old Mr. Ratner that hung over the cash register.

I really wanted to learn what to do, how to eat, talk, act, seeking self-confidence the only way I could, from the outside in. But I was tormented by doubt and embarrassment. I suffered bourgeois afflictions that must have come from my mother, and the desire not to be downtrodden by convention, which came from my father. My mother was a slave to rules she wasn't sure of; my father knew there were rules and he loved to break them; my grandmother didn't even know rules existed.

Occasionally Esther spoke to me, addressing me brusquely in rapid-fire Yiddish. Coming here at sixteen but never learning English—this was her up yours to the New World. Was she really trying to communicate with me, forgetting I didn't know Yiddish? Or did she care so little that she had no memory of what I knew or didn't know? At my look of incomprehension, her expression would turn to disgust: What use is this child, if she can't even speak? *Feh*—she would dismiss me with a wave of her hand. I felt as though I was nothing more to my grandmother than a body sitting on the aqua padded chair, a body with no one inside, much as I felt with my father. And like him, if I had appeared before her without my parents, without those usual clues to my identity, I knew she would have been unable to place me.

My dying father, who lacked example of love, whispered to me: I had an aunt and I never saw her.

An aunt? Whose sister? I asked.

My mother's sister. My mother had a sister, he said.

I knew he meant that she had a sister here in America, because whomever she had left behind in Europe he would never have expected to see.

What happened to her? I asked. Why didn't you ever see her?

I thought he would say, I didn't see her because she died.

Or, I didn't see her because she moved away. But he didn't say anything at all.

I waited for him to speak. As his silence extended, it dawned on me that something was wrong. Was he sicker, had speech finally failed him? I reached up to the bedside cup to offer him a drink of water. When he spoke, I understood that it was not his illness that stopped the words. When he spoke, his whisper was choked, as though the words themselves had been stuck in his throat, or even deeper down, in his heart, too sticky with secrecy to be dislodged easily.

I never saw her because my father was sleeping with her, he said.

He pushed the words out with effort and then he sobbed, and by the strangled sound of his sob I could tell that this was a big secret in his life. My feet turned cold and my skin was tingling and there was a swirly darkness around us, like lots of little wild spirits let loose, whispering, turning, and diving.

I asked him questions, one after the other, without waiting for their answers: What happened? How did you find out? Did you know when you were little?

He said, I didn't know until the day my father died. He was in Columbia-Presbyterian Medical Center, up in Washington Heights, near where we were living at the time.

My father spoke, as he often did when referring to events or situations that occurred during my childhood, as though I were a friend or a stranger to whom the story he was telling would be real only through his words. He did not speak as though I was an adult who once had been a child in the same house he lived in. Always when he did this, the ground slipped under my feet, and for a moment I was blotted out of my own life, the tree falling in the forest that no one is there to hear. I wanted him to know that I remembered, that I was there, that I, the very same woman now holding his hand, had been a child standing outside the hospital on the sidewalk; it was cold and windy as I waited for him to come down from a visit to his father's room. I wanted him to know that I knew many things about that hospital. Half the people in our apartment building worked there— including my mother, for one long, terrible summer. I wanted him to know it was the person he was talking to right now who had, one morning, walked past the open bathroom door and seen him crying silently while he shaved, and who had asked my mother why and she had said his father died last night.

I know, I remember, I said.

I went to visit my father every day, he continued, but my mother was always there. I was never alone with him. I think she didn't want us to be alone. Then one morning my mother didn't come, and that was when he told me. He died that afternoon. It was as if he kept himself alive until he could speak to me.

Every word of what my father said next was tightly wrapped in pain: The thing is, it was not just my aunt but it was other women, and with my mother, other men. I had an uncle, too, my father's brother, but I never saw him either.

I had a million questions, but I asked none of them. My father was having such difficulty speaking, the subject seemed to be exhausting him, and, besides, what he had already said was apparently the nub of what had really gone on in the basement apartment on Brighton Third Street between Max and Esther, and that was enough for now. There had never been anything specific, anything that was named or, so it seemed, that even could be named, behind the thunder and lightning of the storm that had crashed and rumbled in that basement. That my grandparents had hated each other was all I knew. To say they didn't "get along" was, as my mother would have put it, "the understatement of the year."

My grandparents had been presented to me as two wild animals hunting each other in a jungle of incompatibility. Why had it never occurred to me that deeds, specific, hurtful, vengeful acts, were at the bottom—in fact, had to be at the bottom—of such predation?

I had assumed, without really thinking about it, that they had played by conventional rules, which would have forbidden illicit lovers—and, certainly, brothers and sisters-in-law. I was shocked, I had to admit, though really I should have known that hate would have needed to have its engines stoked to continue to burn as hot as theirs did. I was shocked because they were poor, they were Jews, they were neither glamorous nor even attractive. Why had I never imagined them seeking solace and revenge beyond their own four walls? After all, anyone can find a place to hide, a moment to hide in, under the boardwalk on the cold sand, in the back of the store. It can always be done.

Inside this shock there was another, deeper one, one that also, now that I knew it, seemed inevitable: my father and I had both grown up in families controlled by a shameful secret that was kept from us. These secrets had been our blindfolds. He couldn't see the shape of the hate in his house, and I couldn't see the shape of the despair in mine, even though we bumped into them everywhere. We had no stories, no circumstances, just depression and hate that seemed to have no cause, no solution, no end, and no beginning.

I felt my father's terrible shame. He was still under the

thumb of that old family secret. That was why he was telling it to me, as his father had told it to him, on the verge, at the very last minute. That was why he looked so stricken.

Don't be ashamed, I wanted to say. You didn't do anything wrong. It was them. It wasn't you.

I wanted to say, I know what it feels like to live inside a secret and not know you do.

Let's talk about how it was for you and how it was for me, I wanted to say. I know just how you felt.

I wanted him to say: I see that is what I did to you. I wanted him to know and marvel at this sad but real connection between us. We were members of the same club, but I suspected that he hadn't yet put that together. Guilt, self-involvement, whatever, blinded him from the obvious.

I wanted to say, I'm an expert in the field of secrets. I know how to talk about them. I could do more than give you sympathy. I could understand. But I couldn't speak, and not because I didn't feel sorry for him. I did; I felt sorry for both of us. I couldn't speak because what had happened to me was because of him.

It was true—it was as if a hand were clamped over my mouth. I couldn't talk. Each feeling canceled out the one before: sympathy shut up by anger, anger shut up by awe. Awe at the wonder of the story. Awe that there had been more secrets. Awe at the coincidences in the story we were living out, which did not seem random but like those in a story written by a human hand.

My father said: My mother was a beautiful woman.

I nearly laughed. His mother, beautiful? Was he raving?

I looked at him. His eyes were full of pain. No, he was sick, he was dying, perhaps he was exaggerating, losing perspective, but he was speaking from his heart.

I loved my mother, he said, but she was so bitter. I thought everything was her fault in those days. I always blamed her. Then, when my father told me this, then I could see what he had done to her, how he destroyed her.

I had never thought he might have loved his mother. I thought he had known not to, as I knew not to love him. But he had. Suddenly it was as plain as day; it explained a great deal. He was still that poor little boy, caught in the trap of love not returned, and so all his life he dreamed of her as beautiful and sad. But nothing could convince me that she had been beautiful or that what he felt for her was love. He had longed for her affection, and he thought that meant he loved her. He blamed himself, that he was not worthy, and he blamed his father, no saint, clearly. He had lived a dangerous illusion that in some way was at the bottom of all his troubles. If only he could have given up this mistaken perception long ago. It had warped everything in his life.

He was dying, but I wanted to shake him. Truth! truth! I could have yelled at him, is what is required if you, I— anyone—wants to move on, and this is not truth, it is a jumble, a mush. She was not just a victim. Listen, I spent time around her. She was sour, impossible to swallow. Bitterness crackled off her skin like electricity, keeping us away. Only anger and vengeance could bloom in her scarified heart. You couldn't have found love with her, no matter what.

I wanted to wake him up. Don't you see, I wanted to tell him, that a mother can be betrayed in the worst way and still not reject her child. Not unless the stage is already set for that twisted twist of twisted plot. Your father betrayed her, but it wasn't only that which made Esther push you away. There was nothing wrong with you. There was something wrong with her.

I wanted desperately for him to see that what I knew about his mother held together, made sense, didn't shred in the fingers, like what he said about his father destroying her, which fell apart the minute you examined it. I wanted to rip away his fantasy, his hope that if the cards of her marriage had been shuffled differently, she would have loved him.

I couldn't do it. It was impossible. He wasn't ready. He'd be hurt and baffled. And who was I to decide what was love and what was not? Yet I did know, I was sure about this. He might glimpse the truth like an eye opening for a second, but then the eye would shut. He was going to die, so he would never be ready.

I wanted most of all to pull him back to where we had been not more than a blink ago. The Geiger counter that detects delusion had stopped ticking when he told me he had never for a moment in his life seen me as a separate being. But we had left that place, and now there was nothing to say. I breathed the thick, strange aroma in the room, the odor, I suddenly realized, of death. The smell of death filled the air, books say, and I had doubted them, but here it was, I was breathing that air for the first time, and—not for the first time—the books were right.

My father's death smell was easier to breathe than his usual smell. During an acid trip early in the 1970s, he experienced a flash of insight to the effect that covering up the natural smells of the body with deodorants was one of the immoral madnesses of the modern age. He told me about it afterward, how he had realized: How can we do this to ourselves, how can we believe we stink because they tell us we do? He threw his Mennen Speed Stick into the trash and never bought another. He showered every day and said that worked fine. He was right; it was obvious. I tossed my Queen Helene deodorant stick into the wastebasket in the bathroom of my Bennington dorm. It seemed too personal to tell him I had done so, but it was a gesture of solidarity nonetheless.

My problem with his smell started a few months later, when he began using cologne. Acid had made him aware that deodorant was an agent of repression, that we had been brainwashed into thinking our breath and our armpits smelled bad so that Procter & Gamble could make money. Advertisements preyed on our secret fears that we are unattractive, soiled, spoiled.

My father's adoption of cologne worked against a different set of strictures. Cologne had been off limits to men (except for one or two acceptable brands, like Old Spice and English Leather), just like pastel colors and necklaces and makeup and long hair. In the 1970s, when dashikis and beads and bright, ugly ties appeared, my father continued to wear his uniform of a denim work shirt, khaki pants, and a black beret, but he joined in the rebellion by using cologne. His being was powerfully enhanced, his physical presence enlarged. Less than ever could I stand his touch, his nearness. I gagged on his strong smell; I held my breath when he came to hug me.

He left an olfactory pawprint on everything he touched. When he visited, the house was permeated with his aroma. When he left, I'd tear the sheets off his bed, holding my breath, feeling like a madwoman. Stuffing sheets into the wash, adding bleach, opening windows, airing out the rooms, horrified at my horror of him, telling myself: He is the only person you have this reaction to, so you are not completely crazy, you are crazy only when it comes to him.

I gave this disgust some thought. As far as I knew, nothing really bad had ever transpired between me and my father. He never hit me, and he never approached me in a sexual way.

It's true that I got a bigger dose of my father's body than I wanted. In the mornings my mother and I came out of our rooms either fully dressed or wearing nightgowns and bathrobes, buttoned up and tied tight. Nothing sexy or provocative for us. Flannel nightgowns, terry cloth robes. Aaron and my father paraded around the apartment in jockey shorts, summer and winter. Sometimes an undershirt. My father's large, hairy belly protruded over the elastic waistband.

This fat man so barely dressed was not a pretty sight, but we were lucky. I could hear nearly every morning my mother's warning voice from their room: Sidney, put on your underpants. She reprimanded him and he obeyed, slightly annoyed at the bother but obedient, and he was not an obedient man.

Aaron imitated him. This is what men wear around the house in the morning. I suspect he would have been comfortable wearing more, and I know what unease I felt before this display.

Years ago, just after Maury and I started seeing each other, he got out of bed naked one morning to answer the phone. I followed him a few minutes later, wearing a bathrobe, I'm sure, and sat down at the kitchen table, watching him walk around carrying on a long conversation. He saw me sitting there looking at him, but he was not embarrassed. Nor did he seem to be showing off. He was just talking on the telephone in the kitchen, as if he were wearing clothes. This was simply his body, and he felt comfortable in it, as well as comfortable with me. Here was nudity neither flaunted nor shameful, a vision of freedom from that dichotomy, like a rush of fresh air. This was a state to strive for, this was a happy example to emulate. Oh, blessed relief of a better alternative! It might take me a long time to feel such ease, but it burned like a bright light, this simple goal.

One night I had a disturbing experience that forced me to question whether something more overtly sexual hadn't gone on with my father. Something long ago, something repressed. Eleanor was a year old, and the two of us were visiting my parents in Fort Lee. Eleanor and I were sleeping in what used to be my room, on a foldout couch. I left the lamp on so that Eleanor could see where she was if she woke up in the middle of the night. Before I went to sleep, I had been reading a book that I picked up off the table in the living room. It looked interesting. Your father is reading that, my mother said, but he is already asleep. So I took it to bed with me.

Before I fell asleep, I put the book on the floor next to the bed. Some activity in the room, someone fumbling near the bed, half woke me up. The lamp was off, the room was empty. I drifted back to sleep, then woke up again. There was still no one there, but this time the lamp was on and I noticed that the book was gone. It was three in the morning. I woke up fully, very agitated, my heart pounding, overwhelmed by the feeling that something terrible had just happened. Someone had been in the room, that was clear. I felt that Eleanor and I were in serious danger, and I considered that we might have to leave. But it was the middle of the night, I didn't have a car, and we would have nowhere to go. Besides, what was I so scared of? I couldn't be in any real peril. Still, this ominous feeling would not leave me. I stayed awake the rest of the night, nervous, watching over Eleanor. I won't come here alone again, I concluded. Whatever this was about exactly, I didn't want to feel that fear again.

What I figured out had happened, and what was confirmed in the morning by my mother, was simple. My father woke up, looked for his book, came in to get it, turned off the lamp, thinking I had left it on by mistake. My mother, whom he had woken up, saw the light go off down the hall and, knowing I wanted it on for Eleanor, came in and corrected my father's error. That was all. Nothing ominous in the least. My fear was a visitation from the past, when there had been real danger in my days and my nights. A kind of flashback, aroused by the disturbance in the room. This made sense to me and was easy to understand. What was more difficult to fathom was the very realistic vision I had had, when I awoke, of my father in his underpants standing in the doorway, masturbating while looking at Eleanor and me asleep. This could have been some sort of blip on the screen of my mind, some weird image activated by the events of the night, or it could have been a ghost, something that once had happened and now had returned to make itself known.

Eventually I concluded that what I had seen was not a memory revisited but something more symbolic, like a dream image resonating from reality, containing truth but not literal truth. I considered it for a long time and checked with myself about it now and then, just to be sure. He lacked empathy, he overwhelmed me, he idealized me and hated me, all ingredients from a recipe for an incestuous dad, but I had no sense that he had been one, not even a sense of a sense. I made myself think about it. Over and over, I tried to sneak up on myself with it, knowing I was afraid of what I might find, knowing that I might be good at hiding from myself what I did not want to see. I waited for feelings and images to deliver a hidden message, but none did. Finally I completed the investigation and closed the case. It was a relief of sorts to have been forced by the vision to grapple with the question. For years it had lurked in the back of my mind and sometimes charged to the front, as when I was loath to breathe in his smell or to touch the sheets on his bed. It would have been an obvious explanation. On the other hand, my brother, who had abused me, scared me but he didn't disgust me. My father, I concluded, disgusted me just because he was disgusting. I felt lucky; one kind of incest is enough for anybody.

No wonder my mother was bitter, my father croaked harshly. She was a strong woman, ambitious. What could she accomplish in that world where all she was allowed to do was clean and cook? She was smart. What kind of life was that for her?

When I was in college, I read *Sisterhood Is Powerful*. I insisted that my father stop calling women *chicks*. My mother read Betty Friedan, threw a plate against the wall, and said, I hate this whole domestic scene. She, who had been holding a full-time job for years, insisted my father learn to wash a dish and do a laundry. She joined a consciousness-raising group in Manhattan, declaring that if he wouldn't drive her to the weekly evening meetings, she would go by bus and subway, a long and not necessarily safe journey. He took her; he sat in the car and listened to the radio, and then he drove her home.

At first he resisted our arguments, but when he heard about a group of men meeting to talk about feminism, he went along. The other men in the group were psychologists, sociologists, the kind of men my father had never personally known but had always considered effete, isolated from reality. They told him he was amazingly intelligent. They pushed him in front of television cameras and microphones. He was a natural. He was on radio and television talk shows; he was featured in newspaper articles. He was the token working man of this movement, with his Brooklyn *deese* and *dose* and not even a high school diploma.

Seeing him on TV, I'd think: This man is brilliant, this man has charisma, this man could have been a great teacher. And sincere, very sincere. He believed deeply in the feminist analysis of men and their ways. He tried to practice what he preached. For the first time in his life he became aware of the domination we had screamed at him about for years, complaints that had fallen on deaf ears. Now he tried not to interrupt, to listen. He tried to "get in touch with his feelings," a phrase which now sounds more than trite but which, when it was new, accurately conveyed an emotional activity that had had no name. He tried to open up to others with kindness, a bit of consideration. He developed sympathy for men he had always scorned, like my Uncle Simon, the meek, ignorant barber, whom he wouldn't even grace with a hello before.

Seeing him on TV, I'd think: What a waste, what a thing he could have made of his life. And I'd feel proud that he was making something of it now, something worthwhile. And I'd feel angry because there was this sham to it, that he allowed himself to be thought of as Joe Average, when in fact there was nothing about him that was average, except his income. Who he really was, was hidden. The drugs, the jazz, the stacks of books he took out from the library and always had, books of essays and history and political analysis. He presented himself on TV as a simple guy, a union man, a regular dad, a regular husband. It made his message effective, it made me crazy with frustration, and it also made me laugh.

You shmucks, I wanted to say to the commentators, do you know who you are talking to? This isn't Archie Bunker, not even a left-wing Archie Bunker. You're speaking with an ex-junkie who reads William Burroughs and Rebecca West and C. P. Snow and loves Charlie Parker and takes LSD. He was never an average father or a typical husband. He's in disguise, and he'd better be, or he would never get on your show.

After I was about thirteen, when he had stopped using heroin and was at home more, he would sit in an upholstered chair in the living room on weekends and evenings, biting his nails, picking his nose, eating, and reading. He followed my mother around the apartment after they got home from work, reading aloud to her. He would burst unannounced into my room, book in hand, insisting: Listen to this, it will only take a minute. And no matter how I protested, he would read to me, his voice a paroxysm of excitement at the brilliance of the analysis, the description, beating me about the face and neck with the blazing lamp of truth and art.

Stop! Stop! I would cry out to his deaf ears. But I was proud that in that rinky-dink New Jersey town where no one read anything but *Reader's Digest*, my father read real books; he read the *New York Times* from cover to cover, and he did battle with it, wresting his own opinions and conclusions from its facts, reading between the lines, sniffing out what was missing, inconsistent, covered up. His intellectual energy was a lightbulb that was always on. Who did he share it with? My mother, who skipped all the complicated philosophical discussions in novels, and me, a kid overwhelmed by his torrent of words.

The men's feminist movement offered him a platform for his natural charisma and a chance to be admired. He learned from it how to rethink history, herstory, to see how his mother had been a prisoner as well as a jailer, had been expected to be satisfied with babies and dishwater and rolling out noodle dough. She had a grocery store but only for a few years, until the family had had the money to buy a house. She had no education, no skills, just her natural, unfocused brains. It was a narrow life into which women were bent, forced, and stuffed. All this was true. But, essentially, my father was still groping for excuses.

I was impatient with my father's evasions. My grandmother had been too damaged to love her son, though that constitutes its own kind of excuse. Can you blame damaged people for their misdeeds? Can you blame them for not changing? It is a difficult problem. What if the very part that contains the ability to repair the damage is broken? Or, perhaps worse, what if what is broken is the very part that desires change?

I am in my thirties, married, living in Cambridge. My father calls me up and tells me he has just finished a new poem and he's mailed it to me. It has two endings; he's not sure which one is better. He'll be calling me back in a couple of days to hear what I think of the poem and which ending I think is better and why. Meanwhile, how's everything?

Before he started writing poetry, he had never tried anything that didn't come easily, which ruled out almost every activity but reading, talking, sleeping, and eating. True, he had learned to trim windows, but he was somewhat artistic, and the mechanics of window display are not complex. His writing involved him in all the struggles he had never engaged in, all the strategies he had never preached: practice makes perfect; perseverance furthers; if at first you don't succeed, try, try again.

Giving up or never trying had always been the way. Words but no action, no accomplishment. You cannot fail if you do not try. If you succeed, you are lucky or it was easy, or an accident, or, in the deep recesses of my father's mind, something worse. In the middle of my senior year in college, in a fit of anger he accused me of having cheated my way through the previous three years of school. In fact, the opposite had been true. College was a monumental struggle for me. From the first month, when an assignment was handed back to me with the comment, You don't know how to write a paper, I had to face the fact that I could no longer slide through as a reservoir of untapped potential. I had to learn how to work, to expose myself to criticism from those whose opinions I could not discount, a task at times so hard I nearly broke.

By writing poetry, my father for the first time dipped his foot into the pond of trying. This was a different sort of risk-taking, different from the shooting-up-in-an-alley kind. This was a more constructive sort of derring-do, not an all-or-nothing proposition but an average sort of thing. It was part of the changes he was going through, a kind of maturity that had come out of being in the men's movement. When a person has been, how would you say?—unformed, un-normal, living strangely or dangerously?—watching him grow up and even grow out a bit has a tremendous drama. What will happen? Will he make it? What form will he take?

He was changing in certain ways, but he had not changed much toward me. That would come later, if at all. I knew that. His blindness to me would be the last blindness to be lifted, if ever. I had my own problems, and talking to him was like pumping a bellows on a steady blaze; when I talked to him, my problems, my insecurities and anxieties, flamed up and threatened to consume me. What should I do?

He calls me before the mail comes to see if the poem has arrived. He calls me later to see if I have read it, and if I haven't, he reassures me in a too-hearty voice, It's okay, take your time, I know you are busy. He calls me the next day, eager for my comments. I try to forget but cannot forget that he never asked to read a poem of mine all those years before, when I was writing and he was not. I tell myself I am being petty and small, but my annoyance with him grows with each poem, with each call.

For years I assumed that therapy would help me to learn to accept my parents, my father especially. I imagined I would become, through self-understanding, less vulnerable to the wild rage that swept over me like a forest fire, a monsoon, a force too big to stop, to put out. I was nineteen the first time I went to talk to someone, the college psychologist, a kind, skinny, bug-eyed, middle-aged woman, who met with me every week in her barren office on the top floor of Commons and listened to what I had to say about my rage at my parents, a rage I didn't understand at all. I met with her and it was good to talk, but she couldn't really help me, except that she did, simply by listening to me. My friends listened, but they too were riding waves that tossed and crashed over their heads, and the caring and love we gave each other, remarkable and helpful though it was, was like talking to oneself in the end, not to another. Mrs. Flory was an other, an ear, listening to me alone. I couldn't *not* talk; I had to let some of the steam inside me out, into the air, where it formed itself into words that, though incomprehensible to me and to her, were hung out there like a crazy painting or a book that kept trailing into gibberish but still could be looked at, observed. And that cooled me off. A bit, only a bit, but that was better than nothing.

Then came the day, in my senior year, when I returned from winter work term and went to see Mrs. Flory and I said, I found out last week that my father was a heroin addict when I was growing up. And I cried and cried and cried so hard and so long that I knew I would be crying for years and trying to figure everything out for years. But it was a momentous time, the beginning of my narrative, the first words of a story that might make sense.

The parts of the story were all around me, words flung on the floor, the gibberish I had been talking, but the difference was that now I might be able—I had to be able—to pick up the words and put them together with other words, memories, feelings, and they might, they had to, make sentences, make a history, make sense. It was the beginning of a long journey in which I stood still, or rather, I sat still, sat at a table with all the pieces of the puzzle, and put them together when I could, slowly, failing, succeeding, but never getting up. Meanwhile, of course, I lived. I worked and fell in love and moved from here to there, but all the time I was sitting at the table, fitting pieces, turning them around, the life I was living becoming part of the puzzle as I lived it, part of letting me see who I was.

I was joined at the table by therapists. There have been seven all together, three seen only briefly, and only two who really mattered. But they all changed me, and I was gradually, very gradually, like a snail edging ahead, less willing to be pushed around by Aaron and my father. It wasn't that my father pushed me around by demanding I dress a certain way or work at a certain job. He was equipped with a wind machine that sucked me in, this man who talked and talked and talked and wanted approval and encouragement and support and to be listened to and admired. And had no other terms. That was it. Not because he said, I have no other terms, you will do what I wish, but because he simply had no other terms. He needed what he had not been able to give, and his need was huge, but so was mine. I needed him to give me something, and after several years of fooling around with the puzzle pieces, I saw that I needed him to say, I'm sorry. He wanted me to be his dear friend, but he was going to be, until he said those words or their equivalent, my enemy.

Finally I said, Stop sending your poems to me. It is hard for me and I cannot be your teacher. He was hurt and startled and wanted to know why. How did I explain it to him? Did I say, It's about being used, about not getting anything back? About me drowning in your words? About you not noticing me going under? About your What do you think of this, What do you think of that—questions you ask and ask and ask?

My father turned to me, a look of yearning on his face, and asked: Where could I have learned to be a father, to have a family?

He answered himself: Not in that house. Not in that inferno of anger. Not there.

Inferno of anger. I felt in that phrase the fire that kept him alive as a boy and that later pulled him toward death. The crackling in his chest must have been so loud he could hear it, and he must have tried to put his hands over his ears to stop it, but that didn't work. He needed something stronger, more systemic, because it was the sound of his heart.

I didn't know details, but I always felt the bulk and blackness of what happened to him in his childhood, how he had been lost in it as in a dark, scary wood. I felt the evil in the basement, scene of the crimes against him. Nameless, shapeless crimes hit against my brain. I felt how the basement had been his prison, his torture chamber, though I don't know what his torture had been. I always felt lucky that I wasn't him, because if my childhood had been as bad as his had been, I feared I wouldn't have been able to stand it. I wouldn't have been strong enough. I was afraid my mind would have cracked, as I suppose I felt his in some way had.

My own circumstances were good, compared with my father's and Aaron's. That's what I believed. I diminished my own suffering to believe it, but it was nevertheless true. Their childhood sufferings were held up to me by my mother as icons of misery so terrible that what they had gone through and were going through excused all their excesses. They were not responsible for themselves because of their mistreatment. This was a belief I never questioned. It was my mother's belief and it became mine. I believed in it the way other children blindly believe in God and do not dare, even in the secret recesses of their hearts, to question his existence. To claim that my sufferings held a candle to theirs would have been blasphemous.

In my mid-thirties I joined eight other women and two therapists to sit in a circle every Thursday night for twelve weeks, in a basement room at Massachusetts General Hospital. Each of us qualified to be there because we had been sexually abused as children. That was all we knew about one another when the group started, except that each of us was also in individual therapy—a requirement for entrance into the group. Over the weeks we discovered another commonality: everyone else's stories sounded worse to us than our own. I can't believe that that happened to you, someone would breathe. Oh no, the speaker would say, what happened to you was so much worse. We could not stop normalizing our own experiences, though none of us normalized the terrible tales of the others, which we felt right down to our bones.

I stared at the window next to my father's hospital bed. A few years ago, a thief entered the apartment through that window, stole some money and my father's cigar box full of hashish, which is what he was really upset about losing, since he had enough in the box to keep himself going for a few years, but he couldn't tell the police about it, of course. We laughed about that on the phone, imagining him saying, Officer, get the bastard who stole my hash.

The hill outside the window was a piece, a scrap, of the Palisades, "the cliff," as we who lived on it called it. My parents' apartment building was built into the side of the cliff, which is miles long and runs along the Jersey side of the Hudson, towering, steep, unclimbable on the river side, negotiable pretty easily on the more gradual landward side. In the first place we lived in Fort Lee, there were two cliffs, one behind the other, with a dip in between, a paved road running along the dip like a stream. We lived on the top of the back cliff, and I had a view of the cables of the George Washington Bridge from my bedroom. I had walked past the bridge every day on my way to school at P.S. 173 in Washington Heights, so I never forgot that I had been flipped over the river like a pancake, and now I was on the other side. I was looking at the city; I used to look at the cliff. Halfway across the bridge a sign marked the boundary of the territory of New Jersey and the territory of New York: YOU ARE NOW ENTERING/YOU ARE NOW LEAVING. It was a boundary I could see through, a sheer curtain, one side green, with little houses and all white people and few Jews, and sleds and ice skates and white-people food like Jell-O molds and hams with cloves and buttery rolls; the other side coffee cakes with nuts and lox wings and all kinds of face colors and German and Yiddish and Spanish and black from the South and black from the North and poor people and dark smelly corners and gangs of boys who cut up little girls' faces into tick-tack-toe patterns, and hopscotch and tar and asphalt and concrete and bus lights glowing like Christmas lights in the rain.

I had crossed that boundary with all my worldly possessions when I was nine, a chubby girl from the cement world, scared to death of the nature world. I learned about earth on the cliffs. I spent hours climbing and digging, finding fossils, arrowheads, bits of china dolls, ancient bottles. I lay on the warm brown grass above the river, across from the city, and felt myself a deep-breathing speck of life between the deep endless ground and the vast endless sky. Nature and history, people come and gone. Sitting, legs dangling, on the cliff's bald granite top, where there were no houses, just trees and birds and the wide, silver-blue river. Everything as it had been forever, primeval, except for that dramatic backdrop across the river, face-to-face with me, the whole city laid out, piled with bricks and blocks and spires and wires up up up, making a din and thunder too hard to believe I was too far away to hear. Thinking how it must be there, that roar, as a constant in our ears, steady, unceasing, so that what we think is quiet is not.

It was April. Washington Heights is black and white in my memory of that last day, a memory that shows me to myself coming home after school and finding the heavy metal door to our second-floor apartment unlocked. I walked down the long hollow-sounding hallway, first past Aaron's room, then past the bathroom, the tiled kitchen, the dining room, where my parents slept, the living room, and finally my room, and found no one and no furniture anywhere, only emptiness and echoing silence. In my own room nothing but a square of sunlight from the curtainless window, burning white on the yellow wooden floor. I opened my closet door. I had been abandoned. I knew it. Nothing was left of me or my family, except my body standing and staring into the empty closet. I had been abandoned, but what riveted my attention was the interior of the closet. It was triangular. The two side walls met in a V a foot or so beyond where the clothes used to hang. For the three years I lived in this room, I was sure the closet was a rectangle. Its actual shape had been obscured by the clothes. What I believed to be real had not been real. I had had a wall that my eyes did not see. My closet was not what it had been, and it had never been what it had seemed to be. I stared into the closet, and as I stared, it turned into a warm, exciting hand drawing me into the intersection between presence and absence, into and away from life.

I had walked right past my parents. They had been in the car in front of our building, waiting for me, but they didn't see me walk by and I didn't see them. Finally my brother came upstairs to see if he could find me, and there I was, staring at the real and the unreal, the seen and the unseen. He said, Where were you? It's time to go, and I turned and walked down the hall with him, down the stained marble stairs, out the heavy glass front doors, and into the car.

Our first morning in Fort Lee, opening the door of the squat new brick two-family house, stepping out onto the front porch, I am not sure if standing on the porch is allowed, if it is our porch or only for the tenants on the first floor. The spring is aromatic, heavenly. The new green leaves swaying, the sky blue, the sun hot, birds singing, crocuses up—though I do not yet know the word *crocus*—the smell of it all, earthy, grassy, and sweet. I am not in a park, but there are trees towering over me, shadowing the path along which sparkle grass as green as emeralds and little flowers as yellow and purple as jewels. I am in paradise; I am in a new, new world.

The street has no sidewalk, no traffic lights, no people walking. Am I permitted to walk right in the road? There are no cars, so it must be safe. I pick a direction and begin to walk. The asphalt is wavy and lumpy with patches, like a country road in a book. I try to look relaxed. When I have walked past three houses, a girl and a man, about to get into their car, look at me from their driveway. Am I doing something wrong? I panic, wheel around, and walk home as fast as I can, my heart thumping in my chest.

Without Debbie, I would never have gone into the woods, and I certainly would not have learned how to catch snakes and salamanders, how to climb a tree, even if not very high, to leap a stream, even if clumsily, to jump down from a garage roof. Without Debbie, I would not have known what it was to love someone so much that your time with that person is different time, apart from the troubles of life. I had always had friends, but with Debbie, things were different. We lost ourselves in play for hours on end, indoors and out. It felt as if I had never played with anyone before, in the same way it feels, when you fall in love with the right person, that you have never really loved before, that the other loves were rehearsals or shadows of the real thing—the thing you can never know until you have it.

Debbie lived across the street. She was my age, in my third-grade class in school. She was a tomboy, the third of four children. We lay in the long grass on warm days in a spot on the cliff we especially loved, hidden in bushes and tall weeds. There was nothing in front of us but river and sky and city. We ate lettuce leaves and Saltines we had brought for a snack, taking turns stroking each other under the chin, as safe and cozy as kittens.

Debbie wore black high-tops and blue jeans and could out-run any boy in school. She was skinny; I envied her knobby wrist bones and her collarbones as straight and defined as two sticks. In her room she kept such wonders as a homemade balsam pillow and a weightless ball of goose down. We walked as silent as Indians through the woods, imagining the island across the river as they had seen it, flat and green. We had shoeboxes of beads and arrowheads. We'd sit down in the dirt, push the earth around with a stick while we talked, uncovering a small china arm, bent at the elbow; a china head with wavy china hair, white and encrusted with earth we rinsed off at home; a long-stemmed clay pipe, which might have been brand new, except for the dirt. There were spoons and some bones and bottles of wavery glass. We climbed a ladder through time, touching its rungs through dull orange beads, bits of glass.

Her parents and all her relatives were born-again Baptists. Religion permeated their lives. We taught ourselves to use slippery ivory chopsticks sent by her missionary aunt and uncle from Indochina; another uncle directed the Chattanooga Boys Choir. Debbie had to wear a dress and starched pinafore all day Sunday, half of which was spent in church. Her paternal grandfather, a Bible illustrator, built their house with his own hands; they said the reason he suffered a fatal stroke was that he had been painting "the chains of the devil" on a church mural. Debbie told me proudly that she was one-quarter Jewish; her father's mother was the daughter of a rabbi from Philadelphia but had converted and was one of the most fanatically Christian of them all.

They believed that Jews, being unsaved, were inferior by definition. Fortunately for our friendship, Debbie eyed her parents' religion from a cynical distance. She didn't have any fervor. In the summer she suffered through Daily Vacation Bible School and camp meetings that sometimes lasted a week. Her parents took me to church a few times. My mother said they were hoping to convert me, and forbade me to go anymore, but she needn't have worried; I was not convertible. I knew there was no God out there, but only inside.

In fourth grade I developed the habit of pulling out my hair, a habit I soon felt I could not control, which frightened me. I created a sizable bald spot on the top of my head, which I carefully covered each morning with barretted-down hair. I feared the spot would show, and I suspected that sometimes it did. But no one ever commented. As the habit worsened, my fear of it worsened. I could not stop myself from disfiguring myself. The bare spot was getting larger; soon it would be too large to hide. I knew I had to master the urge, or I would soon be stepping over a line that separated the normal from the not normal. To act normal was my conscious, demanding task. I couldn't give it up; if I did, I might never come back. Having a big bald spot on my head meant I would no longer look normal. I would look crazy, and people would treat me accordingly. I saw myself as walking on a narrow path that dropped down steeply on either side. If I fell, I was lost. I decided that I could stop pulling out my hair, that I had to stop, but it was very difficult. My hand went up to my head as I lay on the couch reading (I indulged in this habit only when I was alone), but I resisted the urge to pull. I stopped cold turkey, or at least that is how I remember it, and never started again. I could have—I felt the urge—but I knew that the outcome would be a repetition of the terrible shame and fear I had already experienced.

When I was in graduate school, a teacher I had been working with asked me to tell him about myself. I said I had moved around a great deal as a child and mentioned my father's addiction, my mother's depression, my brother's violence. I told him I felt as if I hadn't accomplished much in my life, that I was still hoping I would, but that it embarrassed me to have spent so much time trying to figure out how to get along in the world and what it was I really wanted to do. I was in my late twenties, getting a master's degree in social work. I felt I had been floundering hopelessly for years: a college degree in literature, a few years of work in publishing in London and New York, writing poems that I never finished; a decision to become a therapist, a year of undergraduate psychology courses at NYU, a year in graduate school for psychology at City College. Moving to Worcester, Massachusetts, with Maury for his residency in family practice, working for a year as a proofreader, going to Boston University's School of Social Work, where I was then enrolled. Still writing, but still not liking what I wrote. Being in therapy since I was eighteen years old, and still needing to be. I didn't tell the graduate school teacher that I suffered from panic attacks in cars, planes, subways, buses, that at that very moment I was barely hanging on to our conversation as I battled waves of terror. We were flying down to Washington, D.C., to deliver a paper we had written together, and I had to keep monitoring my breathing and relaxing all my muscles even as I was talking to him, just to get through the flight. I felt like a mess. You should be proud of yourself, he said. That made no sense. Of what should I be proud? I was a failure, a person with potential who had done nothing of any importance, a disappointment to myself and to friends and teachers who had believed in me.

I moved to London with a friend after I graduated from college, the spring I found out about my father having been an addict. I wanted to be far from my parents and figure things out. There was a gray haze in front of my eyes all the time, the haze of sadness. It was a veil that I hated and wanted to pull to the side, like the veil on a hat, but I couldn't make it budge. It was between me and life, cobwebs that were thickening. Every Wednesday afternoon I left my job early and took the tube to Highgate, walked up the hill to a modern apartment house, and looked at my watch. If it was four o'clock, I rang the bell; if it was earlier, I waited outside, even in the rain. There was no waiting room, no lateness, no first names, and, most surprising of all, no tissues. I raced frantically for the Northern Line, I stood outside in the rain, and after the first few sessions, I brought my own tissues. Her face was pleasant, small featured, and sharp. She was in her fifties, and a Scot. Dr. Millicent Dewar. Her hair was white, and her kneecaps shone white through her stockings. Her wrist bones were fine. She kept white china birds on the windowsill, two identical birds, one facing the other. We met in her apartment in a room lined with books. One of them was called *On Becoming a Person*. When my eyes rested on that title, I cried. I told her about the steep drops on either side of the path on which I walked, about the gray haze, about my family. Miss Miller, she said, in her dignified, clipped voice, I have heard about much more terrible families than yours, but never one as confusing.

I had stood on the corner of Palisade Avenue and Whitman Street, waiting for the light to change. I was in fifth grade, on my way to school, and I knew I was confused. I was confused about everything, every single little thing. My head was buzzing with confusion, my mind was a maze, with dead ends everywhere. Go and stop, go and stop. I wanted to lift out my brain and put in a new one.

My father said, Give me that, would you? He waved his hand toward the bedside table. I pointed to the water glass, the box of tissues, but he shook his head no. The only thing left was the TV remote control. He nodded vigorously when I touched it; his fingers itched for it impatiently. This was absurd. He was dying. Was he really about to turn on a football game or the latest episode of *Mystery?*

He hit the rewind button with his shaky hand. The VCR whirred. It was a tape. What is it? I asked. Just something I want you to see, he said. His voice was excited. He straightened his neck and stared intently at the screen, which was still black. He may have been eager to replace our real-life conversation with a tape, but I wasn't.

I'd rather watch it later, after you're dead, I wanted to say, but to say no to him, a dying man, seemed wrong. And it had always been so difficult to change his direction. I felt overcome with inertia just thinking of it. The hated passivity washed over, turning me to mush. I should grab the remote out of his weak hands, I thought. It would be easier than grabbing a rattle from a baby. I should say, Forget it, I don't want to stop talking.

I should at least say, I won't let you start the tape until you tell me what it is.

I was worried that the tape was the one of him and a small group of other men filmed last year over the course of a weekend they spent talking about their sexual histories, their sexual lives. My father had been invited to participate on a project to make a television documentary featuring men of all ages and persuasions speaking frankly to one another about sex. The last I had heard, it was being edited with an eye toward broadcast on PBS.

Dream: I am in my bedroom, lying sick in bed, wearing a nightgown and bathrobe tightly tied. Maury and my mother are sitting there in chairs, talking. They are fully dressed. My father comes in, takes off his clothes, and gets into bed with me. I pull the covers up around my neck. He doesn't cover himself, but lolls naked, fat, smooth, like a huge baby. Maury and my mother don't seem to mind this, or even to notice. The bed is large, the queen-size one I sleep in every night with Maury. My father rolls around but he doesn't touch me. I tell him to get out of bed and put on his clothes. He doesn't listen. I shout at him. He doesn't listen. I push him off the bed, shoving him away with my feet until he lands, laughing, on the floor. There he continues to laugh, only now he is grasping one of my ankles in each hand and gripping so tightly that it hurts, and I cannot withdraw my feet. I kick my legs wildly to shake him off, but his grip is like a bulldog's. He will not release me. I feel rage in his hands but he laughs and jokes as he strangles my ankles. Don't be so uptight, he teases me. Finally I break free, only to run into him later in the hallway, dressed. I am enraged and tell him so. It's wrong for you to get into bed naked with me, don't you see that? Don't you ever dare do that again, I say.

I am spitting with fury. This time he doesn't laugh. He hates me, too. I feel hate radiating out of him to me. Then he says, What are you making such a big deal out of this for? Why are you so goddamn uptight? Relax a little, would you, for God's sake!

What is it? I asked again. I really didn't want to see that film. But he said only: It's great, you'll like it. I want you to see it.

I turned toward the TV, helpless. It was positioned atop a bureau directly opposite the bed. That room was my father's cave. It was my mother's room, too, but she just slept there, kept her clothes there, lay in bed with my father at night and watched television. Otherwise, she inhabited the living room, while he lived primarily in the cave. It never seemed sunny, even though there was a big window. Maybe it was the hill outside the window that made it seem dark, even though the hill rose gradually and didn't block out the light. The blinds were hardly ever pulled all the way up. And apart from the framed posters of Billie Holiday and Charlie Parker, it was nothing but functional. Their bed was just a metal frame, mattress, box spring. There was the ugly tan vinyl recliner, the secretary desk stuffed with my father's writing, the heavy, inexpensive bureaus my parents bought when they got married. And, of course, the TV. My father watched a great deal of TV in the last years before he died. Basketball and football games, old movies, public television documentaries, and C-SPAN, which he said had convinced him that those who govern our country are more competent and intelligent than he ever imagined. When the illness he didn't know he had began to exhaust him, he spent countless hours in that recliner, biting and picking while the

TV fed him the information he needed to live, like an IV affixed to his brain.

I was curious about the sex tape but I didn't want to watch it with him. I felt pinned, like a victim of torture who is in suspense about the next method that will be applied. If it was the sex tape, would I insist he turn it off? If he didn't, would I leave the room? Or would I just sit there and squirm?

There's a famous psychology experiment in which each subject was ordered to give shocks to a victim whom the subject could hear but not see. Unbeknownst to the subjects, these victims were confederates of the experimenters. The victims sat in enclosed chambers partitioned off from the subjects' control panels. Nearly all the subjects cooperated; nearly everyone kept obediently upping the dosage, despite the victims' screams from behind closed doors.

A film of this experiment was shown in one of my psychology classes. I knew when I saw it that if I had been one of the subjects, the experimenters' orders and white laboratory coats would have meant nothing to me. No, I would have said, I can't do a thing like that, give shocks to someone for no reason, and most certainly not just because you tell me to.

The subjects who followed orders wanted to please the scientists. You could tell by looking at their faces that they were proud of their ability to overlook the suffering of their "victim" in order to be judged and to judge themselves good, obedient citizens who were able to surmount their personal discomfort and moral doubts for the higher good of science. Obedience for its own sake held no attraction for me, so it would have been easy for me to refuse to give the shocks, easy for me to find and maintain my moral footing. But what if, I asked myself, the experiment had been designed to study the ability to handle pain, rather than the willingness to inflict it? What if the experimenters had told me that they wanted me to sit behind the door and take the shocks, to see how much I could bear? I would have felt a pull toward participating in that experiment. I would have had an interest in finding my limit, in proving my bravery. I would have known that this was a sick experiment. I most likely would have said no, but I would have felt drawn to saying yes.

I had come to see that my pain gauge was improperly calibrated. I had worked for years on fixing that gauge, sitting once a week across from a woman whom I had hired for a general overhaul. When we discovered the defective gauge, we homed in on it as central to a great many other faulty functions. After all those years of work, the gauge was functioning better than it ever had, but I still wasn't sure when to say, Stop! Enough!

II

My father died three days later, in the late afternoon. That night my brother and I were sitting at the table in the dinette. My mother was asleep. All three of us were exhausted. We had been taking care of my father around the clock, waiting for him to die.

Outside, the trees were hidden in the darkness. The lights of New York City were blazing across the river. I couldn't see Manhattan from where we sat, but I knew it was there, buzzing, humming, crackling, bright white spangled with yellow, green, and red lines and dots of light. The noises of cars along Palisade Avenue and the lights from the high-rises, set one after the other along the cliff in a neat single row, were nothing in brilliance or volume compared with what was roaring and shining across the river. I knew that the million lights of the city were shimmering in the river water, sparkling like diamonds, jewels spread out each night for those of us in the dark woods to feast our eyes on.

Aaron and I had been calling people to tell them my father was dead and to let them know that the funeral would be tomorrow. We had in front of us my parents' address book and one of my father's old pocket-size "books," in the back of which he kept the numbers of his clients and his friends. Until recent years he bought a new book every January, its wine or black soft leather cover stamped with the year in gold, its whisper-thin eggshell-blue pages edged with gold. There were always colored maps of the world in the front of the book, on thicker paper, and pages of facts on population and capitals and temperatures. He kept the book in his back pocket, usually with a rubber band wrapped around it a couple of times, to help hold it together, and when he took it out to consult it, or to schedule a trim, which he sometimes did at home over the phone, he'd transfer the rubber band to his wrist. He had to wet his index finger several times to get purchase on the tissue-thin pages. By the end of the year, the edges of the cover would be worn and the book itself bent to the shape of his body sitting in the car and kneeling in the windows.

Almost as soon as he died, we started making phone calls, in order for people to make plans to come to the funeral. Jews bury people right away, so that the dead can return as quickly as possible to the earth from which they came. As Aaron and I made phone calls, a man—I assumed an old man, wearing a *tallis*—was sitting in the closed-for-the-night Gutterman-Musicant funeral home in Hackensack, in a room with the dead who were awaiting burial, watching over them and saying prayers. So the dead would not be alone.

Aaron and I had finished our calls. Aaron was smoking a

cigarette. I wished I still smoked, that I could let myself smoke. This was the perfect moment for a cigarette. The red-and-white-checked vinyl tablecloth, the toaster cover with the appliquéd rooster, the cheap brown wall phone that crackled with static, the uncomfortable but indestructible wrought-iron chairs we sat on, everything was stubbornly still there. Aaron and I were there, too, my father's children, all grown up.

Aaron said, I'm worried I'm like him.

Anger had a way of seeping into Aaron's every word, not necessarily directed at anyone or anything specific, but then again it often was. Aaron always sounded irritated, about to walk out, slam the door, screaming, You stupid fuck!

Now he sounded just sad. It's marijuana, Aaron confessed: he smokes every day. It's the only thing that makes him feel better. He thinks he is addicted. He's tried to stop but he can't. He hides it in the barn and smokes it there because he doesn't want his wife to know.

In a lot of ways, I said, your situation is worse than mine. I was the victim, so I have the luxury of feeling wronged, to think of myself as innocent. But you don't even have that.

He shook his head, looking down. We'd been through this before. I was about to tell him what I always told him, that he could feel better if he got some therapy, that I feel so much better because of therapy, which means there is hope, there is a way out.

He'd always come up with reasons he couldn't see a thera-pist—he didn't have enough money, he lived too far out in the country, he worried that his friends or business connections would find out and think badly of him. These reasons cut no mustard with me, as I always let him know. I was like the capi-talist who had worked from the bottom up to become CEO:

anyone can do what I did with just a little pluck and determination; your obstacles are nothing but excuses; you have to be willing to help yourself.

How can you stand to feel the way you do and not do anything about it? I asked. It was a question I'd asked him before. This time he had a different answer, one that was not an excuse, one that finally made me see why he—knowing he needed help, knowing he suffered, knowing he could be helped—did not rush to get help.

What he said was: I'd rather feel the way I do than face what I'd have to face in therapy.

Once, when we were teenagers, we happened to come home at the same time late at night. As we stepped into the apartment together, there was a whirring, and a shadow darker than the darkness flitted past us into the living room, dimly lit from the streetlight outside. Pretty Bird must have escaped from his cage, we said, but when we turned on the light, there was our parakeet, sitting demurely on his perch, his beady eyes following the strange bird as it swooped frantically, looking for a way out. A screen had been raised a few inches on one of the windows, probably by my mother when she was shaking out a dust cloth; that was how the bird had come in. We waved our hands, trying to direct it to that window, but the bird only became wilder.

I'm not sure why the scene struck both of us as funny. Maybe it was our own helplessness, our surprise, Pretty Bird calmly observing the ineffectual activity of the wild bird and of us humans. We collapsed on the floor, unable to move, laughing ourselves sick. After a while one of us made some vain attempts to help the bird, shooing and talking to it. But that only got us laughing even harder, which woke up my mother, who called out to us from the bedroom. When I started to open the door to my parents' room, the doorknob came off in my hand. I staggered back to Aaron, holding out the knob, unable to speak for laughing, tears running down my cheeks.

It was around the corner from the table where we were sitting now that we had slumped against the wall that night, weak with laughter. The night of the bird Aaron and I were happy together with nothing but laughter, no fear or tension scuttling between us like electricity shooting across wires.

Therapy works, Aaron, I said. It really does work. All the bad that happened really happened. You've already experienced it; it's already part of you.

He shrugged, but not out of indifference. I have to stop banging away at him with my right reasons, my right answers, I realized.

I can't do it, he said. It's just the way I feel.

This was how it was, this was how it had always been. He couldn't imagine himself as anything but lost, and I always saw myself as on the way to being found.

Just out of college, terribly confused about what I should do next, I went to see an old man, an astrologer, near Bloomingdale's. He had a beaded curtain and an Aladdin's lamp on his bookcase, and he held my hand and looked at my palm and talked for two hours. He said, You are from a very pessimistic family, but you are an optimist. You must get free of that pessimism. It is not who you are.

Many years later my therapist said, If you had inherited your mother's depressive personality, you might have committed suicide as a child.

My brother used to talk about killing himself; I used to think he might drive off a cliff. I'd picture his faded-blue

Volkswagen bus going over the edge. Maybe he once said that he was thinking of committing suicide by driving his car off a cliff. I don't remember. By the time my father died, I no longer thought Aaron would kill himself. He had stopped talking about it, and I didn't feel that rock-bottom desperation from him anymore. But the bargain he was talking about struck me as another kind of death, an unbearable death in life. He thought he was making a reasonable decision, avoiding the fire by staying in the pan.

Debbie and I crawled under the trees that had been chopped down that day in the woods but not yet cleared away; they were lying piled on top of one another, their leaves still green. We crawled under them, along the ground, where it was dark and hot. After a while we wanted to get out, but so many trunks had fallen crisscross that we were disoriented and didn't know which direction to crawl to reach the opening where we had entered. We looked for other openings, but the edges of the pile were impenetrable. It was hard to breathe in that still, hot place. Then Debbie started to sniff. Air, air, I smell air, she said. There it was, a trickle of spaciousness, of freshness in the suffocating dark. We followed it and came to an opening. We climbed out, scraping our arms and legs, laughing, crying out, Air, air, I smell air.

Aaron is only nineteen months older than I am. Now that I have children, I know how close in age that is, how hard it is to take care of one child, and how much more work it is to take care of two. I know how hard it is to deal with jealousy, sharing, quarreling, hitting. I have learned that doing nothing is a choice, that even doing nothing is not easy. Nothing is easy when your children are small, not even the wrong thing.

Aaron is handsome. We look alike: thick, light-brown hair, hazel eyes. His nose is aquiline, with pronounced depressions above each nostril. Our maternal grandfather had this nose. I saw it every day in the old framed photograph of him in his stiff, high-collared Russian army uniform. We took this photograph with us each time we moved, and set it up on top of a bureau or bookcase. To my eye, the imperious, mustachioed, square-jawed young man in the photo did not look like the poor, conscripted Jew that he was but like a self-important, dashing member of the Polish or Russian aristocracy. He had played trombone in the czar's band, so he was treated relatively well. When he came to this country, he had to find another trade; his teeth were bad, he lost them, and he could no longer play. Eventually he became a fur cutter in the garment district of Manhattan and a martinet in his home in the Bronx, ruling his family like an officer whose pleasures are tinged with sadism. His four children feared him deeply, for the bite of both his tongue and his belt. My brother looked strikingly like him. I looked like my brother but not like my grandfather. I was rounder faced and softer featured, like my maternal grandmother, a clever, gentle seamstress, who died before I was born.

My brother was a skinny boy; I was chubby. My mother poured heavy cream on Aaron's Wheatena in the morning, but he was indifferent. I was the one who wanted it. I could have sipped the cream straight from the carton and sometimes did, if no one was there.

Aaron was nervous, jiggling his leg when he sat. He often looked scared or angry. Sometimes when he was hurting me he looked so cruel that, later on, I recognized the blank, transported expression on the faces of film actors playing psychopaths who stalk, torture, and kill. I no longer see such movies. I used to go and pretend to myself that I wasn't as scared as I was. This was an old trick of mine, one that was difficult to unlearn.

My brother wasn't much of a talker. I was full of words; they ran like rivers through my head and out of my mouth all day long. I struggled thoughts into words. Words dried in his mouth, like sawdust. He didn't like their taste. Making ideas did not absorb him. He tried, but the vines of confusion grew over each thought so fast that he lost his way, couldn't go ahead or back on the same path.

His fingers were sure. He could make things, build intricate models: cars with each tiny engine piece glued on just right, or big sailboats with perfect rigging. He could follow the plans and not make mistakes. When he was a teenager, he taught himself to play the guitar. His delicate fingers moved over the strings, hour after hour. He hunched over the guitar, one foot up on its toes, nervously jiggling, his long brown hair fastened in a ponytail, a Lucky Strike hanging from his lip. His music wasn't melody, it was a cascade of notes, shimmering in the air, boring to me because it was so unfocused, fascinating to him. Neither of us could carry a tune. Maybe if he had been able to, he would have made real songs.

He didn't do well in school. Schools in the 1950s were very rigid. Handwriting had to be straight, spelling had to be correct, and if they weren't, you were not trying hard enough. He was a lefty. He held his pencil in the proper grip but tilted the paper and brought his whole arm around it, encircling the top of the page. His elbow rested on the table, not at his side. His position was awkward and so were his letters, though you could read them.

His biggest problem was reading, and it was a problem

that never went away. Each word was a hard, unyielding knot of letters. To read a word, he had to pry it apart, slowly. Faster, faster, everyone wanted him to speed up, but he just couldn't. Sentences were thorny branches. Books were forests of thorns. Sometimes I was his magic sword. Sometimes I read to him. I swam into the words; their sounds were the ocean I could float on endlessly, weightlessly, stopping only when my throat was so dry I could no longer speak. We read *Call of the Wild* together that way, for a book report he had to write. Humiliated as he was that his little sister had to read to him, still he became swept up in the story; we were swept up in it together. We had a hard, flat, tufted couch, like a daybed, and he lay on it, his head on a bed pillow, listening. I sat at his feet, a pillow between my back and the wall, my feet dangling over the edge. I wasn't afraid, though the wind and the wolves howled. We were, for us, happy.

We moved every couple of years for reasons, unbeknownst to us, related to my father's addiction. After a few months, each new school gave Aaron an IQ test, hoping to figure out why he was doing so badly in nearly everything but math. After the test, school officials would call my mother in and tell her that he had gotten very high scores. They would tell her he was very smart. They would tell her he had a bad attitude. He is rude, they would say. There is no reason, they would say, looking at his scores, for him to be doing so badly. He obviously isn't trying hard enough. They would say to her, He has to work harder. Then they would say the same thing to him. It was like telling a crippled person to walk, but the school officials didn't know he was crippled; they didn't know that the letters didn't look the same to him as they did to them or to me. They just said, Get up and walk, because they thought he was normal.

The way he was smart in math and in building things didn't do him much good at home. Our parents valued reading, talking, and arguing. They lacked interest in making things or fixing things. They recognized his ability but left it alone. His talents were unexpected, even freakish. It was the goyim who fiddled with broken toilets and car engines; Jews called the landlord or the plumber, and took the car to the garage. Who could be bothered with such dull details of life? No one spelled this out, but it was as much a given as the fact that Jews might be Democrats or socialists or Communists, but never Republicans. A Republican Jew might exist but would be a traitor, whereas a goyishe Republican was just an enemy. Aaron's abilities were not criticized, but they were not cultivated. We didn't have tools in the house beyond a hammer and a screwdriver. I suppose it was for him the way it would have been for me in a house without books. No one encouraged the one talent he had, the one thing that was not a problem for him.

He wasn't smart about people either, so he was lonely, and in some of the places we lived, he got beaten up regularly by the hoods. In his early teens he tried to look like a hood, greasing his hair back into a DA, wearing tight, beltless pants. In the morning his pillowcase would be stiff with hair grease. His lids were heavy like Elvis's, his upper lip curled a bit. His mouth was sensual and wide. He spit on the sidewalk, and he walked tough, but he wasn't a hood. The real hoods picked on him because he wasn't one of them and because he was almost always alone.

Long before the hoods picked on him, he picked on me. He fought like a fired-up guerrilla warrior, living for his cause. I had been drafted into this war, which dragged on year after year. My heart was not in it. I would have surrendered, but he never tired of winning.

I almost never took the offensive. Years separated my few acts of defiance. Once I dropped an elaborate model of a schooner he was working on from a second-story window. Once I pushed him—fully clothed, a bowl of cornflakes and milk in his hand—off a dock into a lake.

Once I scared him. I was about ten, and we were, at that time, sharing a bedroom. In the closet of our room was my father's set of golf clubs in their stiff brown leather case, an incongruous possession for a junkie. He never once played golf that I knew of. The woodies had little socks over them. Every time we moved, the clubs came with us. There were golf balls in the bottom of the bag, cool and hard, with smooth saucer dents. I liked their feel against my cheek.

Aaron and I took to putting golf balls around the floor of our bedroom. We must have set up some kind of hole substitutes, like tipped-over shoes or plastic cups. One day, while we were putting, he hit me over the head with an iron. I collapsed to the floor, recognizing in an instant of horror that I might be severely injured. I took stock of my condition; my head hurt, but I was otherwise fine.

Instead of getting up, I lay motionless and pretended to be unconscious. He called my name and shook me by both shoulders. I let my head and arms flop like a rag doll's. I was not even tempted to laugh. I glided effortlessly on the ice of power; it was easy, it was like flying.

Be okay, be okay, he pleaded. Susan, speak to me, he begged. There was panic in his voice, but he didn't leave the room. I opened my eyes just a slit and saw him pacing the big square room, wringing his hands, muttering. I thought, if I were not faking, if I were really hurt, he would be wasting precious seconds that might save my life. Finally he put his hand on the doorknob. He was going to step out into the world of help, also the world of blame. He must have been terrified.

I called out to him in a weak voice and fluttered my eyelashes, as though I were just coming to. Instantly he was on his knees beside me. His face was lit up with joy. What was the source of his happiness—that I was alive or that he was free of the finger of guilt? Whatever it was, I was triumphant. I had reduced him to a quivering wreck; now he was openly grateful to hear me speak, thrilled to help me sit up, happy I was living and breathing.

What I did next was like jumping off a diving board into water that could just as easily have been shallow as deep. What I did was dangerous, and I knew it. I said to him: I was pretending; I didn't really pass out.

He might have killed me for making him squirm with fear and for watching him squirm, for making him happy to see me alive and for witnessing his happiness. But I was lucky. He was impressed by what I had done; he viewed it as an accomplishment. You sure fooled me, he said. He looked at me proudly, and under the admiring beam of his eye, I became thrilled with my achievement. I had totally fooled him. I had terrified him, without physically hurting him. He was impressed by my prowess. Wow! he said. You did a really good job.

In movies, gangsters are fickle. One minute they forgive, the next they blow off heads. There is no way to predict their reaction. I expected Aaron to be angry, maybe even furious. So why did I reveal the truth? He didn't suspect my duplicity; I handed it to him on a plate.

I was the victor for mere seconds before I returned the crown to him, putting him back in control and giving him an excuse to beat the shit out of me. I returned us to our familiar roles: he the frightener, I the frightened. I don't know why I told. When I think about it, this is how it looks: I am out on a pier, walking away from the shore. It is foggy and I am afraid of being on my own. When I confess that I have tricked him, I am back onshore, no longer alone. That is all I know.

I am nine, ten, eleven, twelve. I am standing at the window, looking at the rain. I am standing at my open closet trying to decide what to wear. I am in the kitchen about to make lunch. Aaron comes up behind me, grabs my arm, and twists it behind my back, pressing down hard on my upturned forearm.

The pain is instantaneous, searing. My knees almost buckle. You give? he asks. Yes, I say. There is nothing we are fighting over; the giving in is purely and simply to his power. Are you sure? he asks. He is teasing, mocking. Yes, I say. He presses harder, tightens his grip. Are you positive? he asks. Yes, I'm positive, I say. I know the litany, I know what he is doing, I know my response. This happens at least once a day. What always surprises me is the pain, how much of it there is.

Are you sure you're sure? he asks. Yes, yes, yes, I say. He yanks my twisted arm up. My arm might snap, my mind might snap. There is a blackness of pain edging all I see, like an etched-in frame.

Are you absolutely positive? he asks. On a good day he will stop before this. On a bad day, bad for me, he will go on and on.

Eventually he drops my arm, lets it go limp. It is over, and I still have my arm. I can get on with what I was doing. I can peel the hard-boiled egg and mash it with mayonnaise. I can take down my red blouse and check to see if it needs ironing. This was just an interruption—like when you need to pee, you go into the bathroom and pee and come out again and get back to what you were doing. That's the kind of thing it is—just a nothing thing. Sometimes he stays around to chat with me when it's over. Or sometimes he leaves.

As I pass him on the way to the kitchen to get myself a glass of milk, he jabs out his foot, shoe on or not, and kicks me in the shin. He smiles at me, a superior, satisfied smile, with a slightly beseeching edge. He smiles that same smile when he slams me in the arm with his fist on my way past him. These are casual encounters, a kind of greeting, a reminder that this is a toll road and he is the collector.

We have skits. They are unwritten, never discussed, only performed. Aaron is the director. When he decides a skit is about to get under way, I have no choice. He tells me which skit we are going to do only the instant before it begins. All the skits have nearly the same plot, similar characters, and the same lesson. His character is always an army officer, either Japanese or a Nazi. It is always World War II and I am always a prisoner, a minor member of the underground. I am never heroic, I have little or no valuable information, and I am always afraid.

Aaron pursues each skit the way a religious devotee approaches a holy ritual performed hundreds of times before. The ritual is so filled with meaning that each time it is undertaken, it is fresh and immediate to the devotee. Aaron never lacks enthusiasm for the skits, always throws himself into them fully, although in other parts of his life he is often disaffected, listless, restless, or unfocused.

The officer has the prisoner in his power. He wants a confession. The prisoner is willing to confess, but there are two obstacles. One is that she knows very little of importance; that is, basically she has nothing to confess. The second obstacle is that the officer will not accept her confession. This is when she realizes she is dealing with a sadist. He wants to keep torturing. He wants to show her, over and over again, how helpless she is. It does not matter if she is innocent or guilty, if she is harboring war secrets or not. He wants to torture her; the information she might or might not have is secondary, merely an excuse.

The prisoner contemplates her situation. The officer has made her willingness to confess into a pointless gesture, since confessing—giving in, surrendering—has the same consequence as resisting and being brave. Both result in torture. He deals with her as a resister even though she is not resisting, even though she is already broken. She cannot surrender any more than she already has. She has to face the fact that if she had resisted, if she had been brave and refused to give in, she would not be suffering any more than she is suffering now. She thinks that if she had resisted, at least she would have been proud. Then again, if she had resisted, she would never have known that the torture was inescapable; she would have thought she brought it on herself.

The prisoner tells herself that she has done all she can to save herself from pain, that the pain the officer is inflicting is not her fault in any way. This is not a comfort, exactly, but it is the closest thing to comfort she can come up with.

The officer's words, the prisoner's words, the torture itself, each has an educational purpose. Aaron is trying to teach me— I am acting the prisoner, I am the prisoner, and I am observing the prisoner—the meaning of cruelty. There is dialogue in the skit. It is never spoken out loud, but I hear it clearly in my head. These lines are silently spoken by Aaron when he is the officer, and they are addressed to the me who is the observer of the skit.

The officer's lines go like this: Pay attention now. I am going to show you how someone really cruel acts. Don't you think that this officer I am portraying is a terrible man? Aren't you glad you are not really at his mercy? Aren't you glad that this is only a play? I want you to pay special attention to how little influence anyone has over someone as cruel as this officer. Notice how the officer does what he wants, as though the victim does not exist in her own right. He pays no attention to what she says. That erases her reality; to him she has no reality except as the outlet for his urges. It is precisely that inability to sympathize that is the essence of cruelty. I am showing you this so that you will recognize cruelty in case you should ever encounter it. You are lucky I am showing this to you, so that cruelty will never take you by surprise. It will be to your advantage to be familiar with it so that you can recognize it. I am doing this skit for you, to enlarge your understanding of human nature. Not everyone gets such an opportunity.

The skits were never brought on by an argument. Aaron started them for no reason apparent in the immediate circumstances. He never seemed angry at me when he was doing a skit but, rather, very intent and actually happy, even joyous.

In the skits I always got hurt and could never fight back effectively. There wasn't any way that I could, physically. For instance, when my arm was being twisted, I tried to kick him with my heels, but to get any swing with my foot, I had to step forward—since he was directly behind me—and doing so put my arm into an even more painful position.

One skit was a karate demonstration in which he played a sadistic Japanese officer. The success of this skit depended on speed. It had to be done with lightning quickness or else I might be able to escape or to protect parts of my body with my hands. If it was done well, which it invariably was, I could not possibly defend myself from the rapid-fire karate chops. The skit was announced by a shout of *Combo! Bang! Bang! Bang!* Karate chops hit the nape of my neck, my chest, back, stomach, the base of my spine, in rapid succession. He would get me in the neck; I would hunch over to protect myself, but he was so fast that the side of his hand would get me in the chest. *Bang!* he cried out with each blow. He swarmed all over me, the hard sides of his hands smashing me here, there, up, down. His arms were like the bars of a jail, trapping me, allowing no escape until he was finished. He was gleeful, he was having fun. He hardly ever had fun. His life was lonely, angry. When he attacked me, he had a good time.

Another skit he announced: Chinese Water Torture! I tried to get away before it began, but he grabbed me by the leg as I headed for the door. He dragged me down and climbed on top of me. He sat on my chest and pinned my arms down by holding my wrists against the floor. His knees pressed into my shoulders. I could not heave him off, no matter how hard I squirmed and kicked. When he finally had me where he wanted me, the action slowed down and our characters took over. He luxuriated in his moves, like a cat in the sun. He had me; I was his.

Ha! he would laugh, a villainous laugh. *Ha, ha!* He gathered up a wad of saliva in his mouth. He always had lots of saliva, spitting big gobs of it on the sidewalk like the tough guys whose swagger he tried to imitate. He leaned over my face and let the saliva drop down. Just when it was about to land, he sucked it back in.

You give? he asked. Yes, I said. The saliva descended again. I flopped my head from side to side, so if the saliva landed, it wouldn't hit right in my nose or eyes. You sure? he asked. Yes, yes, I said. Again he got the saliva to hang, just above my face, and again he asked, You positive? You absolutely positive?

My biggest problem was not the saliva but his bony knees jabbing into my aching shoulders. Leaning forward over my face put his weight on his knees, and they bored into me, threatening to wedge their way right into my arm sockets, separating my shoulders from my trunk like a doll's arms pulled out on their rubber-band connectors—the difference being that my arms, once out, would never snap back in. Mine would be pressed off my body by his knees; mine would be pushed away from the rest of me forever.

The glistening glob hung above my nose. I knew the saliva was supposed to be a humorous touch, that it amused the writer of the skit. I admired the great control the officer had over his saliva. He was a master at dangling it, not letting it break off. During the hundreds of times we did the skit, it never landed on my face. The clever thing about the saliva was that it was a distraction. A spectator walking in would think that, all in all, what was going on was not so bad, since no pain was involved. It was a slightly disgusting but silly torture, nothing more. What the onlooker would not have been able to see was that the real torture was being inflicted by the pressure of his knees on my shoulders. That was the real joke of the skit, its real twist. The skit's name camouflaged what it was.

The point of this skit, its lesson for me, was that things can look not so bad to someone else but be terrible to the victim. It was hard for me to absorb this lesson, because I was in such pain. In desperation I would try to go outside the skit. I would try to talk to him in words from the real world, the world in which I was Susan and he was Aaron, the world in which my arms were breaking off. I told him that it hurt too much. Every time we did this skit, I tried this technique. And every time I tried it, I was sure that if he was made aware that my arms might really come off, he would be frightened and he would stop.

But one of the problems I had was that it was hard to speak. Severe pain cuts off the voice. I learned this by experience. In my mind's eye I saw a prisoner in a real cell; I saw nails being pulled off; I saw skin puckering under the tip of a red-hot cigarette. I knew that if, in the middle of the torture, the victim caved in and wanted to confess, her voice might not work. When she was asked, And now, do you give in? she might not be able to reply so as to be understood. If she could not tell her torturers that she gives in, they would be unaware of her willingness to tell what she knows, and the torture would continue, now unnecessary, though only she would know that.

Stop! Stop! My arms are breaking, I managed to say, but it didn't work. He continued to bear down and he continued to ask, Are you absolutely, completely positive that you give? I was amazed, every time, that he was willing to hurt me this badly. I was filled with wonder that he wasn't frightened of really injuring me. After a while my mind started to chop up, to break apart in chips and blips, dark spots and white spots, and I would think, There has to be a way out of this, there has to be a way out of this, but I couldn't think of what or how.

Always, at last, there was a way out. Suddenly, for some reason, the time was up, the skit was over. At some point he always stopped; he got off my chest, he climbed off my body. I sat up, moved my arms. They were there, nothing missing or broken. I was grateful—grateful that he had stopped when he did, grateful that I was not in pieces, grateful that it was over, grateful that the pain had stopped. I was a fortunate girl.

I was grateful that my brother had such tremendous self-control that he was able to stop even though he was having such a good time, even though he was totally absorbed in what he was doing, even though he was not worried about me—even though he was transported. He didn't kill me or wound me, although I could feel his urge to do so as strongly as I felt my own pain. I knew it could not be easy for him to stop, to rein in that urge. I was grateful for his self-control. I owed my life to it; I would have worshiped it at an altar, I would have offered sacrifices to it, anything to make it stronger, to make sure that next time it would be there.

I believed that Aaron and I were acting out the same drama. *Believed* isn't even the right word. Maybe no word exists for what you never question as being real but then later find out was not real. Even now, all these years later, I can hardly believe that we weren't thinking the same thing at the same time during those skits, which were as well-rehearsed as the Rockettes' routines. It is still difficult for me to unwind the gauze of text and subtext that bound us in my mind so closely, to release the skits from the world of unspoken words I thought we shared.

I asked him. I was in my late thirties when it dawned on me. No, he said, I didn't think of myself as an army officer, I didn't think I was teaching you a lesson. I didn't really think at all.

He didn't think of himself as engaging with me in a complex play-within-a-play-within-real-life; he wasn't teaching or acting a part. To him we were not characters but ourselves. The skits satisfied something in him that was very powerful, so he did them over and over again; but he had no words for them except for the ones he spoke out loud: You give? You positive? You sure?

He made up the skits but I made up the roles and the settings. I could not look at what was happening full in the face; it would have been too much, like staring into the sun. The roles were flimsy, but I made them strong. I thought he was teaching me lessons he believed were valuable, making him not cruel, only misguided, and making his intentions good, even benevolent, though he caused me to suffer.

Aaron and I also had regular fights. We argued and hit each other in the heat of a dispute. The skits were formal, cold-blooded, but our regular fights were ruleless and fought with no holds barred. In these fights I sometimes managed to get in a good kick or punch, which I could never do in the skits. Once, I remember, I even made him cry, though I can't recall how.

Scratching, kicking, pounding, slugging—being completely wild, ravingly physical—was horribly thrilling. My body was fully engaged, every particle focused, not a thought thing at all, just visceral. I had to be alert for surprises, for openings; I had to move quickly and strike effectively. I was fighting for my life—that was the feeling. I was also always losing, but that didn't mean I could relax my guard, that didn't mean I could let any opportunity slip by.

The pain had a delicious edge of shock, a waking-up impact right through my bones. It shamed me, this excitement of feeling pain and inflicting pain. There was also shame from the powerful and disturbing intimacy at the height of battle. I knew his pain when I kicked him, because I felt it when he kicked me. I hated him and he hated me. Inadvertently I made a funny face, a grimace of rage or pain, and he laughed and imitated the face, and then I laughed, thinking maybe the fight was over. But while I was laughing, he slugged me, so the laughter was real but also a trick I would later play back on him, and if I did it well, he admired me and raised his eyebrows and said, Well done. I dropped my guard while being praised, and that's when he would slam me again.

The soldier in the jungle is terrified that he is going to get shot. He doesn't want to die. His fear is the same whether he does get shot or whether he does not.

I thought my parents knew. I never told anyone until it had all been over for years. In college I talked about it, but I gave myself no sympathy. I was alive, I wasn't maimed, so it couldn't have been so bad. My brother used to smother me, I would say, and laugh. My brother threw me down the stairs. Those I said these things to listened, but because I laughed, they thought, like me, She is not dead, she is not crippled, she is laughing, so it couldn't have been so bad.

Each time I didn't die, I was not reassured that the next time Aaron would pick the pillow up off my face or let his fingers go loose around my neck. Once he went after me with a knife. It wasn't a big knife, just an open jackknife, but he chased me down the hallway with it, not laughing at all, but really chasing me, saying, I'm gonna kill you. I ran as fast as I could, being a pudgy seven-year-old, and got to my room and slammed the door, but he pushed hard from the other side and got his arm in, and in his hand was the knife. He jabbed the air with the blade every which way. I had to hold the door as far shut as I could; if he got in, he would stab me. I felt the strength of desperation in my body and also the miserable weakness that the sudden strength was augmenting, but how long would that strength last? I braced myself against the door and held it and held it, until finally he gave up and went away. He went away but I didn't take that to mean it couldn't happen again. There would have been no reason to believe that I was safe. Instead, this knife incident gave me reason to believe that I was not safe.

The situation could turn abruptly from safety to danger. My mother could say, I have to go next door for a minute, and I would be left wide open, unprotected. I'd say, Don't go, but she'd say, I'm just going next door, I'll be back in a minute. Aaron would go after me in a hurry, because his time was limited. I'd run down the hallway to get away from him, but he'd grab me and I'd fall. Once, my head hit the floor and I saw stars, actual white, twinkling stars in a black sky, just like in the cartoons. I never knew that could really happen, but now I knew it could, now I knew it did. Then my mother would be at the door, turning the key. Aaron stood up quickly, and maybe I did, too. Maybe I told my mother, maybe I was crying, maybe I was silent. My mother already knew that he went after me, and she left me alone with him, so what was there to say?

One morning a few years ago I woke up, or felt that I was awake, and found myself paralyzed. I was lying on my back with my eyes closed and my neck arched backward as far as it could go, a position that had the effect of limiting my capacity to breathe. I simply could not draw a full breath. I was aware that if I could succeed in moving even a toe, I would be released from paralysis, and then I would be able to breathe. I focused all my concentration on a finger, an eyelid, my foot, trying for a twitch, but I could not move at all.

I tried to speak. If I woke Maury, he would help me sit up and I would be all right. But I could not make a sound, not even a moan. Again I summoned all my will and made a tremendous effort to move, but my muscles had greater power than my will.

I began to panic. I was trapped in a dark, airless limbo, unable to see, breathe, or move for what seemed like endless minutes, though in reality it was probably seconds. I had no sense that I would come out of this; I might but I might not.

Suddenly I was released. I could move, speak, open my eyes. Over the next few months I had this terrible experience several more times. My therapist said it was occurring in the hypnopompic state between waking and sleeping and that what saved me was simply time. That is, eventually I came out of sleep enough to move. She said the paralysis I experienced was my awareness of my body asleep, which is an awareness we normally do not have. She also told me that this experience is not uncommon. Awful, but not uncommon.

One time after it happened, my muscles ached for hours, and shortly after I got out of bed, I had a headache, which didn't go away until the afternoon. I assumed the headache and the achiness were from the extreme tension in which my body had held itself when it was unable to move and yet struggling to move. As the day passed, I kept reliving the sensation and fear of the paralysis. I thought, while I was in the shower, while I was driving Max to the baby-sitter and Eleanor to school, What does this experience remind me of? Why is it familiar to me?

At last I realized that it was not the paralysis that was familiar, but the suffocating. Yes, I had experienced that before and not while sleeping. My brother sometimes held a pillow over my face or pressed my face down into a cushion and held me there long enough that I passed into the beginning of suffocation.

When a pillow covers your face, even if your eyes are open, it is like having your eyes closed. At the doorstep of death you don't know if the door will open and you will go through. The thick wadding presses hard into your face, pressing out the light and people and beautiful things like trees and grass and the corners of the room. The cutoff sensation of suffocating is like drowning in black water. The body, the part that is not under the pillow, becomes all there is. You are floating, you could be anywhere, and you experience the edges of your body as though you are outlined. The longer you cannot breathe, the sharper these edges become and the deeper you sink into what they enclose.

In the bathroom at my gynecologist's office there is a poster on the wall across from the toilet. When I go in to leave my urine sample, I look right at it. The poster is a series of questions. ARE YOU AFRAID OF ANYONE IN YOUR HOUSE? DOES ANYONE IN YOUR HOME HIT YOU OR THREATEN YOU? Etc. At the bottom of the poster is a number to call if you answer yes.

I read the questions each time I am there, and I answer no to them all. My home is safe. I also remember the first time I read the questions. First I answered no to them. Then I thought of myself reading this poster at age ten, say. If there had been a poster like this—and such a poster did not exist at that time anywhere in the world—I would have answered yes to every question. I wonder, and still wonder every time I read the poster, if there was any chance I would have called the phone number at the bottom.

In poetry class in college we were taught that poetry is about naming things, that it is possible to say that nothing exists unless it has a name.

Battered child, dysfunctional family, daughter of a drug addict. Before I learned that these terms applied to me, I did not fully exist. I don't love these words; they shout, Pay attention to me, pity me. I had it bad, I had it worse than you. They are not beautiful words; they sound as rough and ugly as what they describe. I also love them. They describe who I am, in the same way *refugee* or *orphan* is descriptive for others. These are poetic words, resonant words. They are relatively newly minted; I am fortunate to have had their benefit.

I was twelve, Aaron was fourteen. It was lunchtime. It must have been a Saturday or Sunday, because all of us were home. We were sitting at the table in the kitchen and my parents were arguing. My father picked up a bottle of milk that was on the table, and he threw it at my mother. He missed her; the bottle hit the wall and shattered. My father had never hit my mother, and he did not throw things. He raged and he yelled but it wasn't his way to strike out with his hands. The milk bottle left the table and flew through the air. I watched it break into pieces against the wall, and I heard the pieces of glass fall to the floor, glass that could have sliced my mother's face, that could have broken her glasses, that could have cracked open her head.

We were a family held together by almost nothing—chewing gum, frayed string. The contraption was already wobbling dangerously. The milk bottle hit the wall, and I sank to a new level of nauseous fear. Now anything could happen. I left the table and Aaron followed me. We went into his room, closed the door, sat down on his bed. From the kitchen we could hear our parents still shouting.

I will never eat with them again, I announced. My conviction was rock-hard. I was on a mountaintop; the wind of righteousness bit bracingly against my cheeks. I knew what to do; I knew what was correct. I was the voice of wisdom; I was justice with the flaming sword. This was the first serious decision of my life. Aaron, swept up, awed by my confidence, vowed he'd do the same.

I will never forget the look in Aaron's eyes that afternoon; stark admiration, as though I had swum the English Channel, as though he could have saluted. Our parents did not make demands, set limits, assign tasks, make plans. No wonder Aaron went along with me; it must have been impossible to resist my effort at parenting.

In reality, we seldom all ate together, anyway. My mother was working full-time now. No one was around to prepare meals; we came in at different hours. Our pledge was therefore mainly symbolic, but as we sat on Aaron's bed, the words felt as if they carried a great deal of weight. Later, when I announced the pledge to our parents, my mother hung her head. She did not protest.

Aaron and I had each other, but we were not friends, even though we listened to 45s together after school. He still hit and kicked me and he had begun confiding his sexual desires to me in graphic language. Girls he wanted to feel up, girls he dreamed of fucking. Talking about sex animated him, focused his interest, as hitting me did. He talked about tits and cunts and told me dirty jokes. I was fascinated, frightened, attracted, and repelled. I never walked away; I sat and listened.

We had each other. We were sitting on his bed. Aaron was leaning against the headboard, his knees up. That was the afternoon it started. He told me he had been waiting for us to do this, hoping for it. He unzipped his fly and brought my hand to it, as our parents, one wall away, screamed at each other across the littered table.

I could leave this out. The only people who would know it

was missing would be my brother, my husband, my therapist, and some friends. Remembering it makes me nervously ill in the pit of my stomach. I don't want to give it words, to shape and form it into a piece of prose. It's all folded up in my pocket. I could leave it there or I can take it out and open it up and look at it. I could describe what I see, or I could put it away. I have looked at it before, but I have always been in a hurry to put it away.

If I do look at it, I can do so only briefly. A scene comes into view, but almost immediately a curtain goes down over it, the way a real curtain goes down over a stage. I cannot see through the curtain, and I cannot lift the curtain again. A glimpse is all I can get.

Aaron said he would rather be depressed all his life than look at the past. I think he must see all that happened the way I see this one thing. It is like a hot stove: I cannot touch it for more than an instant.

I went along. I didn't pull my hand away. He didn't force me. He started it, but I went along, out of my own free will. I was scared and upset, but I didn't stop him. He showed me how to jerk him off, and I did it. Later he showed me how to suck him, and I did that, too.

There is so much I don't remember, so much I cannot get a clear grip on. My memory, always so sharp, fails me or falters badly. I try to look at the scenes, but the curtain comes down. There are things I recall, sensations, moments, but it's all choppy and it's been that way for ages. For instance, I don't know how long it went on. Was it three weeks or three months? What did he do to me? Did he touch me? I'm not sure. I think he did, but I can't conjure up more than a feeling of pleasure, of orgasm. I have no visual memory of him doing to me the equivalent of what I was doing to him. We must have done whatever we did after school, when our parents were at work, but, apart from my vivid recollection of that weekend afternoon, I know only that we did it often, and usually on Aaron's bed.

I remember he had weights and a bench press set up in the basement. I see Aaron take out sexy books or magazines from a secret place behind the wall. I know we did sexual things in the basement, and I remember sensations of acute pleasure and worry that someone would come down and find us, a terrific nervousness, as if ants were crawling over me and I couldn't stop them.

It was a two-family house, and our apartment was on the second floor. The old woman who owned the house was right above us when Aaron and I were in the basement. I was afraid she would come down and find us, that I would suddenly feel her cold, angry, pale-blue eyes on us. She had delicate, pinched, soft white skin; her carefully waved hair was like a doll's wig. She wore old-lady lace-up shoes: navy-blue leather pierced with tiny holes, heels of medium height. Sturdy, no nonsense. She already hated us. I hated being hated, even though I hated her back. The source of our latest dispute with her was that my father had refused to mow the lawn. It would be so easy for him to do, she said, on a Saturday afternoon. I pay rent to live here, not to work, he said to her. I was awed by his boldness, his willingness to be hated. Screw her, he said to us. She hated our loud rock-and-roll and jazz music, our general domestic disorder, and our yelling. She disapproved of us. She looked at me as though I might smell bad, as though I were a disgrace. It would be far worse to be caught by her than by our mother.

I wanted the sex to stop and I told Aaron so, but he always

cajoled me into continuing, though I don't remember exactly what either of us said. Then my memory becomes sharp again. One day my resolve to stop became utter and unshakable. He tried to talk me into continuing, but it was like trying to turn a fish into a dog. I simply would never do anything like it again, I said. I had no doubts, and nothing could make me change my mind. Nothing, not anything he could say or do. What if I make you? he asked. I'll tell Mom, I said. He could see I would do that, that I would tell the world if I had to.

It was as if I had been dreaming and suddenly I woke up, wide awake, fully alert, realizing I was in danger. What woke me up? What I recall is that I got my period, and this alarmed me into waking. We never had intercourse, of that I am sure, but Aaron had begun to talk about wanting to. Things were getting out of control: my body, Aaron.

It was easy to make the sex stop. All I had to do was say no and mean it. Aaron never touched me again. He tried and I reminded him: I will not do that anymore. I don't have to tell you why; I don't have to explain. The answer is no.

If it was that easy to stop the sex, I felt, then the fault for continuing was mine. I could have stopped it anytime.

One day, weeks after we stopped, he grabbed me in the hall and pushed me up against the wall. His eyes were burning. You bitch, he hissed, someday I'm going to throw you into the closet and stick it up you. *Ugh, ugh, ugh,* he grunted, thrusting with his hips. This frightened me. Would he really rape me?

It was good to have control of myself again, although I was stained, besmirched by what we had done. I had never felt the slightest connection with the word *sin* before, but now I did. I had sinned. I was complicit. I was not the victim; for the first time I was not innocent. I was a willing participant. I had wronged myself; I had been irresponsible to myself for the sake of pleasure, even though that pleasure was edged with revulsion and fear. I had stopped swimming upstream, out of the turgid pool of my family toward clearer water. I had always headed that way, and if I was held back, I would start out again. This time I had turned of my own accord and swum back. How could I have betrayed myself so?

When I was seven, an old man molested me in the mail room of our apartment building in Washington Heights. He grabbed me with surprising strength and pushed my hand into his pants. I felt a strangely cool, soft thing. What was it? He pushed his hand up my skirt and down into my underpants. I had been trying to be polite to him; he was like a million old men in my neighborhood, little and bent. He spoke with a familiar, thick Yiddish accent. He said he needed to find someone in the building, but he didn't have his glasses so he couldn't read the names on the mailboxes. If he could find the number of the apartment, he could ring the bell. I was helping him look for the name he mentioned, even though I didn't like him, even though I wanted to go away from him. Then he grabbed me and put his hand in my underpants and made me feel that cool squishy thing. I got suddenly strong and I pushed him away and ran upstairs and told my mother, who said, It's all right. It wasn't your fault. I felt better, and I thought everything was all right. My mother didn't call the police. Did mothers and fathers call the police, in those days, when their daughters were molested? She did say, with great kindness in her voice, It's not your fault. I was grateful to know this, even though it had not occurred to me that it was my fault. Nevertheless, when she said it, I was relieved, and I thought, Everything is all right now.

But if everything had been all right, what happened to me next would not have happened. What happened next was that I forgot the entire incident, totally, absolutely, as if it had never taken place, until I was thirteen and some girls were talking about reading in the newspaper that a girl had been sexually attacked. In a flash, I remembered everything, as though I had just pushed the old man away and had run upstairs to my mother. I remembered it all. Thunderstruck in the middle of a sentence, I said, That happened to me once. Someone molested me. When I got home, I asked my mother, and she said, Yes, it happened, and just that way, the way you remember it. So I know that things that have to do with sex, with taking-advantage-of sex, can be blocked out, even when you con-sciously believe you are innocent, even when you say no, even when you manage to escape, even when you are cloaked in the moral safety of victimization, in the eyes of the world and in your own eyes. Which, with my brother, in my own estimation, I certainly was not.

I was four, so Aaron was six. We were living in Queens, in a garden-apartment complex. Aaron was lying on top of me on the floor in my parents' room, inside a house of blankets we had made, doing something with me I can't remember, something that involved us taking our pants down. My mother knocked at the closed bedroom door and asked, Can I come in? Aaron answered, Not yet. My face turned burning hot. Aaron hissed to me to pull up my clothes, and while we hurriedly did, my mother waited outside the door. I felt her body there, on the other side, waiting, obedient. Only when he shouted out, Okay, did she turn the knob.

My mother trembled in front of Aaron. He cursed at her and called her a stupid fat pig and said, Shut up, fuck you, to her, and she stood there and trembled. She cried when she was alone with me and said, I don't know what to do about Aaron, he is so angry, he is so unhappy, he sees you have so much and he is so jealous of you. I know it is hard for you, but there is nothing I can do.

III

Three years ago my mother moved up to Cambridge to be near us. She lives in a studio apartment in a subsidized housing project for the elderly. Because she pays only a quarter of her income in rent, she doesn't have to worry about money, even though she has very little. She is seventy-six and the happiest she has ever been. She volunteers in a battered-women's shelter one day a week. She and her friends go to concerts, plays, movies, museums. She helps run a support group at a women's center and is a member of another support group of old women, as she likes to call them. She went to the international women's conference in China last year. She is in therapy. She has been in therapy before, but she never really told the therapist much, she says. Now she is facing so many things that sometimes it is as if she is in an emotional storm, memories and conflicts flying in her face, but she grabs them and looks at them, each one of them, and tries to know them.

Sometimes we talk about the past, and when we do, the conversation is different than it used to be. No anger, no blame. Sadness and sympathy, each for the other.

Things are starting to make sense to her, to come together in a pattern. She tells me one day, as we are driving in the car, that she has been talking to her therapist about her brother, Willy. She has been telling her therapist that Willy used to hit her all the time. She never forgot this, but she just put it aside, thought it didn't mean anything. Now she sees that what happened to her she let happen to me. Now she sees that it wasn't *nothing*, that she was terrorized by Willy. She tells me Willy took her to the movies every Saturday. She remembers sitting in the dark theater next to Willy, and every week a friend of Willy's would come down their row and sit on the other side of her. The friend put his hand up her dress, every Saturday. Willy just sat there and let him. Maybe, she thinks, it was Willy himself; maybe she just can't stand to face that and has made up the friend. But even if it was the friend, she says, Willy knew, he set her up, he let it happen. She was just a little girl, five, six, seven.

She says, I let this happen to you. She is appalled. I thought she knew all along about Aaron hitting me; the one thing I was sure of all my life, and that I kept being sure of, was that she had known. And she hadn't. She said she knew that Aaron used to hit me, but she never thought of what he did as anything serious. She wrote off our fights as normal sibling tussles and kept writing them off. Whenever I'd refer to Aaron's beating me up, she would be sympathetic. But she was always sympathetic. If you voiced any kind of trouble or worry she automatically overflowed with compassion. I took her sympathy to mean that she knew. No, she said to me last year, I didn't know. I was sympathetic just to be nice to you.

Last year I wrote an essay about my father, and I gave it to her to read. It was going to be published, and I wanted her to see the essay before it came out. I was worried that she would not want other people, strangers and friends, to read about our family. After all, some of her friends still did not know about my father's addiction—even Lil, who had lived next door to us in Washington Heights. My essay, which some of those people might hear about or even read, would be "outing" my father's addiction, my mother's depression, and my brother's violence.

I thought that nothing I had written in the essay would be news to my mother, at least not in gist. My father tripping on the subway ride with me—maybe she didn't know that had happened, I couldn't recall ever telling her, but she couldn't possibly be shocked that he had done such a thing. What worried me most was that my depiction of her as depressed would distress her. And even though I didn't think my father's addiction should be a secret, she might not be ready to reveal it to those from whom she had hidden it for so long.

What happened when she read the essay was something I had never expected. It was as though her eyes suddenly flew open. That was how I found out they had been closed. She asked me questions: What happened with Aaron? Tell me. I want to know; I have to know.

She was frightened, but she asked. I didn't tell her about the sex part, but it turned out that Aaron would tell her about it himself, a few months later. That opened her eyes even wider. She started therapy, in a free program at Cambridge City Hospital for the treatment of victims of violence. She was the widow of an addict, the mother of two children who had had a violent relationship. She qualified.

But in a way I was right, I said. You did know. Yes, she said, I did know, but I didn't want to know.

For the first time, I didn't feel responsible for her, I didn't feel that I was her parent. I listened without feeling sick with anger, with demands, with frustration at her jumbled feelings.

The other day my mother called me up. Flo is dead, she said. I'm terribly upset. Flo Cohn was Al Cohn's second wife and my mother's good friend. She had been very ill for the past year, so her death was not unexpected. My mother knew that Flo's death would hit her hard, and it did. The week before, we had talked about it. My mother said she loved Flo as a person, but there was more. She and my mother had lived through much of the same history. Flo's first husband, the father of her children, was the saxophonist George Handy, a junkie and a friend of my father. When their children were little, Flo and George lived in George's parents' apartment. My mother said to me last week: How I used to envy Flo. I used to think she had it easy. She had George's parents to help her, while I was all alone. But when she left George, the Handelmans never spoke to her again. That hurt her terribly, just terribly. She never got over it.

Flo, said my mother, was the last one. No one else is alive who can understand what it was like. At the time, Flo and I couldn't really talk to one another. She left George finally because he was sleeping around. She couldn't stand it anymore. But when she married Al and the four of us got together so much, she and I would talk about those times. She didn't have anyone else to talk to about that, and neither did I. It was a big bond. Now there is no one left.

I wanted my mother to tell me more, so I asked questions, I prodded her.

She said, No one in my family understood. I was so alone then. It was as if I was a nonperson. My sister Etta would say to me, So, has Sidney been a good boy? Can you imagine saying that to someone? Can you imagine how that sounded to me? What a way to talk about Sidney, reducing him to a boy. Anger wells up in me when I think of my family. I was all alone in the world. If they had supported me, I would have left Sidney. I asked Theresa to look for an apartment for me in her neighborhood in the Bronx, but can you believe she wouldn't do it? She said, You wouldn't be happy here. She said, Sol's family would wonder what you were doing here on your own. Sol's mother and father and his brothers all lived in the neighborhood, and Theresa saw them all the time. She didn't want me to move there because she was ashamed of me. When Etta and Simon moved to Florida, I had dreams—daydreams—that I would take you kids and move down there near my sister. I never asked her, but I dreamed about it. And then things didn't work out for them down there and they came back.

One thing, though; my sisters always helped me with money. They gave me money when I needed it, no questions asked. Both Etta and Theresa. And that was great. They didn't totally abandon me. I'm not talking about thousands of dollars, of course. But for instance, when we moved to Englewood Cliffs, there was no refrigerator. Everywhere I ever lived there was a refrigerator that came with the apartment. But when we moved in, there was no refrigerator and I had no money to buy one. So I called Etta and she and Simon drove down right away and picked me up, and they bought us a refrigerator. I paid them back later, of course.

No one understood, she said. I knew that, but I also knew that they simply couldn't understand. I sensed that. And because I was so ashamed, I didn't tell other people. Only my family knew and the wives of the musicians. Savina, Flo, and Merlene. But they didn't understand anything about life themselves. So they were no help, except they were help, just to talk to.

One morning when I was about six years old, my mother told me she had dreamed the night before that she was spring cleaning and had taken a rug out of the closet and started to unroll it on the living room floor. To her horror, hideous beetles poured out of the rug. She tried frantically to roll the rug back up, but it was too late. The bugs were everywhere.

My mother often wore a sweater the color of rust, knitted by her sister Etta in strong, heavy yarn stitched into smooth, perfect, even ribs. It had a zipper down the front and two small pockets with flaps that fastened with buttons. This sweater was so sturdy and well made that I wore it throughout college and for years afterward. Iron wool, I called it. It never pilled, pulled, or wore out. It was indestructible in a way that my mother wasn't, a way you could see and touch.

My mother's eyes behind her thick glasses always seemed to be filled with tears. She was soft all over, plump. Her hair was short and brown, wavy when she set it. Her face was round, her nose was round. When she laughed hard, she cried. We would laugh together, giggling until my stomach ached. My mother could laugh even though she was miserable, which was a good thing. She kissed me often; she hugged me a lot. She told me she needed me, that I was her only friend.

She didn't like to cook and thought she didn't cook well.

Her mother had been a seamstress, but my mother did not know how to sew or knit because no one had taught her, she said. She couldn't draw. She was not a good singer. She knew how to keep the house clean but she was not a *baleboosteh* like her sisters, who spent their lives scrubbing and polishing everything they owned. She felt incompetent in nearly every way, as far as the practical was concerned. With one exception: she knew she ironed well. She taught me how to press a shirt without leaving any wrinkles.

My mother took the test for Hunter College when she was in high school, but everyone took the test, you had to, and she didn't, at the time, even realize it was a test for college. She was admitted without knowing she had applied. Her sister Etta, the oldest, hadn't gone past sixth grade. Theresa left school after eighth grade. Willy finished high school, but he was a boy. Here she was, the youngest, in college. She decided to major in German because she knew Yiddish, so German would be easy. She finished two years at Hunter, then dropped out. The war was on, my father had asked her to marry him, and she couldn't think of any good reason to stay in school. If she graduated from college, wouldn't that make Sidney feel inadequate? He didn't even have a high school diploma. Besides, there was nothing she had dreamed of doing. (I was a dope, she says now; I was a dope.)

Sometimes I felt as if I could put my hand right through my mother. Yet she kept going, slowly, taking tremendous effort to do a little thing, but going, going, pushing herself along. It was uphill for her all day and night, toiling, struggling, lying down for a rest, forcing herself to get up and toil some more. Aaron and I were not to be abandoned, no matter what. That got her up out of the chair to make a meal, to sweep the floor.

Sometimes there was a great deal to her; she was not an empty shell. She loved to look at people, on the bus, on the street, in the subway. People are more fascinating than anything else, she would say. They are just as interesting, just as wonderful to look at, as any landscape. She was right; when I looked around me on the subway, the bus, the sidewalk, I saw faces of all colors, shapes, sizes, different-color coats, many kinds of shoes, purses, satchels, paper bags. An infinite variety, everywhere. My mother looked inside people, too, when she could. She was a good listener, full of interest and sympathy, though she didn't think clearly enough to give good advice, and she usually opted for safety over risk. But as a listener, she had no equal.

She would have liked to have more people to listen to, but we moved so often, and my father was so difficult, that it was hard to keep friends. Also, she was hiding his addiction from everyone she met, so that it was easier not to talk to other people at all, or just a little. But as soon as she met a person with a problem, she was ready: listening, intent, head bent toward the other, nodding.

When she turned that sympathetic face to you, you talked. It was hard to resist. And why resist? Who doesn't want a listener? I talked; her sympathy was soothing. I felt important. Her sympathy was also dangerous. If something was hard for me, she urged me to give it up. If there was a matter of disagreement, she urged me to placate.

She was alone so much that she needed news of the outside world. What I ate at a friend's house, what the friend's parents were like, speculation about motives, bad news and good. Sometimes the news led to self-deprecation. So-and-so's house is so neat and orderly, I might report. Or, So-and-so's mother makes the best French toast. Or sews all So-and-so's clothes. Those remarks always pained her, but I was a reporter and spared her no detail, sometimes relishing the feeling of turning the knife. She would vow to become stricter, to give Aaron and me chores, to make us toe the line, so that our house would be neater and we could learn responsibility. Her mouth would form a tight line, her shoulders would straighten, but that was a different person's mouth and shoulders, not hers. She would continue doing the housework herself, or trying to, at least. The couch, the easy chair drew her like powerful magnets. Her body longed to sit, to stare, to sleep. She had to muster great determination to get up, and even then the bed and chair pulled at her. She struggled against their attraction. They were her solace. She was always tired, and a tired person needs to rest.

We talked about motive. Why does Madeline's mother walk her to school, when all the other kids go alone? Why is Uncle Willy so mean? Often the explanations were off base, but the why of others was on the table, open for discussion, along with the topic of how others make you feel. Leslie's mother makes me nervous. She always watches everything I do, I would say. My mother would listen, nod, wait for more. My mother was not an actor in the play of life, she was not involved. Life happened to her. She took no control, but she watched carefully, open to anything. She was lost, unsure, timid, when she was thrust onto the stage, but interested, always interested.

Mrs. Bouton, my brother's second-grade teacher at P.S. 173 in Washington Heights, took a dislike to him when he arrived in her classroom in the middle of the year. She called him stupid, laughed at him, made fun of him. His ears turned red when he was upset. Talking about her at home, he looked tiny, weak, and frightened. My mother said to me, When Aaron was in first grade last year, when we still lived in Queens, his teacher told me how smart he was. He took apart a clock and put it all back together perfectly. He's very smart, though in a way I don't understand, in a way I don't know how to help him with. This teacher he has now, said my mother, is a monster. How can she be so cruel to Aaron?

On parent-teacher night my mother went to school. She questioned parents of other children in Aaron's classroom, sotto voce, out in the hall, or while looking at a poster in the back of the room. Does your child also report mistreatment by this teacher? Yes, some said, but these parents either doubted the word of their child or saw the teacher as an authority who must be obeyed, no matter what. My mother came home to us outraged. She reported her research. How could these parents not believe their own children? she said. It's clear that this teacher is sick, a sadist. I thought, my mother is so wonderful. She would never doubt Aaron or me. To have a parent who didn't believe you was the worst thing I had ever heard of. I had never even imagined such a thing. I was lucky; my mother was so good.

Then she announced to Aaron and me that, while walking home afterward (seven long, dark blocks, wind from the river whipping across the broad avenue), she had come to a decision about what to do about Aaron and this teacher. I waited, excited, expectant, to hear how she would save Aaron. Her voice changed to the other person's voice. As she spoke, my heart sank. I can see now, she said with emphasis, with definition, with finality, that I should do nothing. I will not go to the principal or speak to the teacher. It's obvious that the other parents won't support me. If I say anything, it will only make it worse for Aaron, she concluded.

———

I am, say, eleven. I am sitting on the couch with my mother in our apartment in Fort Lee. It's quiet here next to the river, on the edge of the Palisades, and quiet in the living room, just the two of us sitting as we so often do. My mother asks, Do you love me? Yes, I do, I say. I don't know if I really do. I love my best friend, Debbie, the world we make for our dolls, all orphans, and the world we make for ourselves on top of the cliff with the earth singing under us, through us. At home it is hard and dark and no one helps me the way Debbie helps me. She shows me, the city girl, how to climb a tree. She shows me how to walk feet sideways down the steep cliff, then waits for me at the bottom with her head turned away from me on purpose. She looks away so I won't feel foolish as I slip and trip down the hill, pebbles flying. No matter how much racket I make, she never turns. She pretends she is watching the clouds or she crouches down, intent, and digs in the earth with a stick she has found.

I watch my mother's face swell up with sadness. I hope things aren't too hard for you, she says. Oh no, Mom, I say. Everything is all right.

If only I knew how to encourage Aaron, she says. If only Sidney or I were more mechanically inclined. Poor Aaron, he was born into the wrong family. Not like you; you are so much like me.

My mother smiles at me fondly. I am glad I am not Aaron. In this house I am mind, he is body. I can speak, he is dumb. I am peace, he is war. He is sick, I am well. I am needed, he is not.

I know he hates school, my mother says. Ever since that horrible monster Mrs. Bouton picked on him in second grade.

Calling him stupid in front of the whole class. No wonder he hates school.

I nod. I had Mrs. Bouton myself, in first grade, the year after Aaron had her in second. She hated boys. I was safe because I was a girl, and a pretty and smart and good one besides, but she was scary. Once she pulled down a boy's pants and underpants and put him over her knee and beat his naked white tush with a ruler right in front of the whole class. Another time she pushed a little boy very roughly and the small of his back hit the corner of the blackboard chalk rack. Yes, I am glad I am not Aaron. My life is so much easier than his. Aaron has problems and I, everyone tells me, do not.

I know it is difficult for you with Aaron, my mother says, but he is so angry in his heart, so jealous of you. My mother's cheeks are wet and her nose is red. I can feel that her deeper crying is being kept inside her, like a flood she is holding back, because she doesn't want to scare me. I'm glad she is not crying hard, the way I know she wants to cry, the way I cry in my bed or behind the locked bathroom door. I know she wants to hold on to me as I hold on to my little stuffed horse in bed, and cry and cry and cry; I'm glad she doesn't do that. I have to help keep her from doing that, however I can.

I know the real reason he is angry, she says. It's my fault. I did what the doctor said. He screamed and screamed. He was hungry, that's all. I should have listened to myself, but I didn't have the confidence. I followed the rules, even though I knew Aaron was hungry.

My mother's lips are pursed, her hands are clasped in her lap, her knees are pressed together. I know this is the way she sat in the doctor's office when he told her: Mrs. Miller, your son is not underweight. You do not need to feed him more often than you already are.

She pushes her arm out from her chest, pushing away the book, the doctor. Finally I said, To hell with them all. I started feeding him when he cried, and he quieted right down. I saw I had been right. He had been starving for months.

I've heard this story once or twice before. There is something wrong with it, something that doesn't make sense, but I don't know what. All I know is that when I hear it, the story doesn't sit inside me right. Parts of it poke at me uncomfortably, no matter how I try to shift it around.

He must never have felt satisfied, she says, mulling over Aaron's feelings. He never got the thing he was crying for. He got other things. I gave him attention, I held him, I walked with him, but he didn't get what he needed. He was always difficult, always crying. And I still can't help him. I couldn't help him then, just as I can't help him now.

She is getting dangerously upset. Her sadness is turning into a big black wave. Doesn't she know that by talking about this, she is calling to the sadness, inviting it to come and drown us? Doesn't she know the sadness is dangerous? She's not trying to hold it back, she's just letting it come, as if she wants it here. Stop, stop, I yell without words. Stop talking, change the subject. She's pulling at me with her gentle arms, pulling at me to save her, pulling me under the black, airless water where I can't breathe, just as I can't breathe when Aaron holds the pillow over my face and everything turns funny colors. I've got to get us out of here. I've done it before and I can do it again. I can open my mouth and words will come out and they will save us. They will be our life preservers. We will hold on to them and we will be all right.

I start to talk. I hear my own words and they calm me down. I tell her everything I can think of. How maybe she is wrong about not feeding Aaron enough. How can you really be sure? I ask her. I tell her that other children are hungry when they are babies and probably at least some of them get over it. I scrounge for signs of improvement. Aaron has a new friend. He seems less angry, don't you think?

She castigates herself. She should be stricter, give us more chores, make more rules. I tell her it's good to have parents who give us choices. It makes us think for ourselves, and that's what she wants, isn't it? Yes, she nods, it is. The mood is lightening up as I talk and talk, my mind the ventriloquist, my mouth the dummy. I tell her: I'm fine, and how could I be fine if you are doing things all wrong? If Aaron and I were both having trouble, that would be different. But the way it is, you could just as easily say you were doing things right as you could say you are doing things wrong.

I am making sense and she can't disagree. She is looking better, there is more hope in her eyes, so the worst is over. She is smiling at me, holding my hand, telling me I am the light of her life, that she is lucky to have me.

I did it. I don't know if I lied to her, I only know that my mind has done its work again. My mind is what I can count on, what pulls me through, what gives me words to say to help her. My mind knows how to make words into nets and wrap her up in them and haul her back to light and air. I don't know how it is that, when I am so confused, my mind can keep making sense. My mind is so smart that it even knows that my pitch won't work unless I believe it when I am saying it. I always make my sale.

———

The next time we talked, it was the same, though we'd say different words. She'd get upset and I'd talk and she'd perk up enough for me to feel I had done a good job, that I'd dealt with the emergency. She'd get up off the couch and I'd have a feeling of accomplishment, which was good, but it was shot through with various twisted-together, frightened feelings. So much depended on me, and we always started from zero: my great logical arguments didn't have any permanent effect on her.

I thought it was the content of my arguments that cheered her up, but I see now it was my caring about her, my trying to help her, that mattered. I never convinced her of anything, except for that. I couldn't possibly have been clever enough, sympathetic enough, intuitive enough to change her. She was my mother, I was only a child. I didn't know that my father was a junkie, and my mother, ashamed and worried and dragged down by her life, didn't have the will to change.

My mother often said she was good. She would make remarks about herself such as, They (the teacher, the principal, the landlord, a neighbor) could see right away I was a good person, a nice person. Like all my mother's statements of certainty, this one made me uneasy. And it was the one she made most often. The voice in which she said, I am a good person, was prissy, emphatic, and superior, with a slight tinge of hysteria. Not the voice of self-doubt, of melancholy, not the voice of her true self.

What did she mean by that amorphous word *good*, that word that I couldn't put my finger on, that irritated me, that dragged at my insides, that she spoke with that unconsciously phony voice?

Some people want most to be perceived as good-looking. Others want, first and foremost, to be perceived as smart. The impression my mother needed to make on others was that she was "good." Looking back, I think being good meant two things to her. One was being good like her mother, which meant being perceived as, and genuinely being, understanding. The other was being a good girl, as she had been for her father: no trouble, obedient.

She managed to effect an almost complete split between her assessment of herself as good and her lack of action in situations where to do nothing was reprehensible. Doing nothing in the face of the bad behavior of others did not diminish her belief in her own goodness, and might even have been a prerequisite for it. After all, her own mother had not protected her children from her husband's excessive harshness. As far as my mother knew, she hadn't tried to stop him. My grandmother bolstered her husband (who was never directly cruel to her) and did not fight for her children, but that had not diminished her children's sense of her as being exemplary.

Unlike her rigid brother and sisters, my mother wanted to be a modern, permissive, kind, and loving parent. My brother hit me but she didn't, and she saw his hitting me as not serious, therefore as not requiring a response. She was appalled at her brother's and sisters' strict treatment of their own small children. My sweetly smiling Aunt Theresa, for example, regularly slapped her little son for not eating enough and advised my mother to do the same if Aaron or I refused what was on our highchair tray.

Every Passover we went to the home of Willy, my mother's brother, for the seder. Willy sported a neat brown Hitlerian mustache that suited his fanatical disposition. For instance, he demanded that his children use only two squares of toilet paper per wipe, never a square more. (How did he enforce this? Aaron and I could never imagine.) Neither of my parents had a nice word to say about him. Willy and his second wife—cold, dour, tall, big-boned Edna, who wore side-lacing, custom-made orthopedic shoes as big as boats—were the only ones in the family with a dining room, let alone a table large enough to seat all the relatives. They lived in what my parents and other family members called a "private house"; the rest of us lived in cramped apartments. They had wall-to-wall carpeting and matching brocade upholstery on fake French-provincial armchairs. Willy was a failed salesman whose money came from the inheritance of widowed Edna. It was only because of Edna that every Passover he could usher his poor relations into his split-level for the whole shmeer, from gefilte fish to macaroons.

Every year, immediately after the seder, Willy flung open the cellar door, pointed to the stairs, and commanded, in a no-nonsense, dog-training voice: All children to the basement. Downstairs, right now! The basement was clean but dark, dank, and empty. Just a couple of filing cabinets and old desk chairs. Bare lightbulbs, concrete floor. If you asked, he'd let you use the bathroom upstairs, but he followed you with his eyes until you went downstairs again. He yelled if you didn't close the cellar door behind you.

The seder was an incomprehensible jumble of rushed words; only the food made sense: porous matzo balls rising from golden broth; bright orange sticks of jellied carrot snuggling up to bulges of pallid gefilte fish nestled in lettuce. The ceremonial meal celebrates the release of the Jews from bondage in Egypt; you are supposed to understand its meaning in your own life, but I doubt any of us knew that. Certainly, the irony of the children's incarceration in the basement on Passover was lost on all of us.

The basement was a horrible, boring place to be. We cousins were a motley crew of misfits, each one sour, angry, and depressed in various admixtures. No one liked anyone else very much. Everyone was grouchy, and there was teasing. I was the youngest of them all, and I pleaded in vain to be allowed to sit on the couch upstairs next to my mother, where, I swore, I would be quiet and not bother anyone. This, said Willy, was strictly forbidden.

My mother didn't challenge Willy, yet she sympathized with us afterward, railing against him in the car on the way home. Willy's a louse, my mother would say. He's such a weakling that he has to boss children around to feel good. That phony, my father would say, with his big fancy house. He thinks it makes him a big shot.

I never expected either of them to stand up for Aaron and me. It never occurred to me that either of them might.

My Aunt Etta's husband, Simon the barber, and my Aunt Theresa's husband, Sol the false-teeth maker, were meek men, washed out, almost invisible. No one would expect either of them to stand up to Willy, to tell him, Forget it, buddy. These are my kids and you don't send them to the basement. My father, on the other hand, was never afraid to speak out for his beliefs, though sometimes it was hard to tell his convictions from his annoyances. He could be outrageously rude. For instance, when Etta and Simon came to see us, he kept a book or the *Times* in front of his face, acknowledging their arrival and departure by lowering the book or paper almost imperceptibly, like a minimal, grudging tip of a hat. He found them unbearably boring, he said. At least you could say hello to them, you could be just a little nice to them, it wouldn't kill you, my mother would plead, furious and exasperated. She is my sister and that is important to me, no matter what she is like. That's right, my father would say. She is your sister, not mine.

He wasn't rude to Etta and Simon to punish my mother. On the contrary. It was as though she were left out of the matter entirely, that the issue was solely between him and Simon and Etta's provincialism and narrowness, toward which he felt virulent hostility. Their limitations aroused in him a moral repugnance. Ignorance, in his book, was a voluntary, self-inflicted state. Those who chose it deserved punishment and lack of respect. But he never said a word to Willy about incarcerating us in the basement, and I never expected him to. That was because he was without connection to us. He saw us being marched through the door, but our pain was not his pain. That was his unmentioned, unrecognized excuse for not defending us, just as my mother's was fear.

My mother did with Willy what she often did in our lives. She criticized him behind his back, feeling brave, even defiant, as she did so, but when it came to taking action, she turned mute. She was afraid of him but I didn't know it, because when she tore him apart verbally, she was like a lioness, relentless and fearless. She was afraid of him but she didn't know it, in the same way I didn't label what I felt toward my brother as fear.

That was the pattern. My father didn't see Aaron and me. My mother felt for us, but she didn't help us. She couldn't.

My mother said, a couple of years ago, I was so afraid of my father that even today just the sound of a man's deep voice, even in another room, makes me tremble.

My mother was scared of Aaron in the same sort of half-conscious way that she was scared of her brother, Willy. You can be terrified of someone and not really know you are. Later, when you can see how frightened you were, your previous lack of perspective on fear horrifies you. At the time you know you are scared, but you think you are less scared than you actually are. That's because your perspective is warped. If you have started life with a baseline of fear that to a normal person would already seem quite severe, you get used to it, you don't recognize it for what it is.

You might ask, How could a grown woman be frightened by a little boy who calls her a fat, ugly pig and does nothing much worse than give her dirty looks? My mother was guilty and confused. She didn't know how to handle my brother. And she was used to being afraid.

Aaron hadn't hit me for years, but one day when I was about twenty-three, I was at his place on 14th Street and we were making lunch. He reached up with his arm to open a cabinet, and I bent my head and covered it with my hands to protect myself, like the cover position for duck and cover. I was shocked that this reflex was still in me.

I was living then not too far from Aaron, on Sixth Avenue below the Village. I was used to Aaron calling me up and demanding I do this or that for him—feed his cats because he was leaving town in an hour, or whatever—and I never said no. I never said, It's too inconvenient, or, You are inconsiderate. I didn't even have those thoughts. One day my friend Alix was there when Aaron called and she said, He's so mean to you. And I said, He is?

In the early 1980s my mother gave the first speech of her life, at a NOW conference. In it she presented herself as having been a typical 1950s housewife, silently suffering beneath the myth of being satisfied by staying home, mothering her children, keeping house. She painted my father as a normal, pressured breadwinner, who expected her to take care of the house and the kids. A generic couple with generic kids. The speech went on to describe their subsequent makeovers as feminists: she was now respected by her husband for earning money in her office job, and the money she made took some of the burden off his shoulders, for which he was grateful. Thanks to feminism, he had figured out how to operate the washing machine and how to sauté a chicken. She, in turn, was grateful for his domestic assistance.

Reading the speech, I was astounded to discover she was still keeping the secret, long after it was necessary. The speech was a fiction by virtue of what it left out. I sat next to my mother on the couch, reading the page or two of typed-out words she had read the week before at a microphone in front of a crowd of women. Can you believe, she said proudly, when I was finished reading, that your mother made a speech? That's great, Mom, I said. But why didn't you tell the truth?

I had come to believe in the truth. The truth made you catch up with it. It was the only way. Lies grew over everything and twisted your mind so that you believed things had to be that didn't, and you didn't know what was really necessary. People wouldn't understand, she said, surprised at my question. They'd all be shocked. They wouldn't know how to relate.

She was right, of course. They wouldn't know how to relate. But I didn't know how to relate to this cheerfully censored story, true as far as it went but approaching the delusional in its denial of reality. I wished she had told the truth, which I knew by now, from my own experience, would ring bells for the many women who had been married, in the 1950s, to other kinds of addicts, especially alcoholics—women who, like her, had tried so hard to preserve the facade of normalcy that they partially succeeded. Thanks to them, in my house—and in so many other houses that harbored secrets—normalcy, though in a stunted form, did exist.

In this way, my mother's speech was eerily accurate. She had lived a censored life for so long that she in part experienced herself "as if" she were the normal woman she depicted in the speech. There was a kind of madness, so many years after the lies had ceased to be necessary, in continuing to live the character she had taken on, in speaking in that character's voice.

My father tied my brother, Willy, to the bed and beat him like a dog, my mother told me. My father was so cruel to Etta. He said terrible things to her about how plain she was, how no wonder no one wanted to marry her. Theresa was beautiful and so good, like a saint, so he never got angry at her. He was very strict, she said. We weren't allowed to drink anything when we ate. He thought it wasn't good for us, and I still can't bring myself to drink even a glass of water if I am eating. If we didn't sit up straight, he hit our backs. He'd come up behind us and hit us hard.

My Aunts Etta and Theresa and my Uncle Willy had no sympathy for children, no pity. Theresa gave me a bath once when I was three or four. She scrubbed me under viciously hot water with a scrub brush like the kind you use for a floor. Her iron fingers dug into my scalp and held me under the water so long I thought I would drown, but then she smoothed her glossy black hair back into a bun and rolled down her sleeves and buttoned her cuffs and put on fresh lipstick and turned back into my aunt with the sweet smile and quiet voice.

Sol and Theresa's apartment in the Bronx was very small, in a nondescript walk-up building, in a not-great neighborhood. Yiddish newspapers were spread over the bathroom floor when it was just washed, furniture polished to a gleam; their son, Michael, was quiet as a mouse, clean as a whistle, pale as a ghost, good as gold. Sol, the false-teeth maker and stamp collector, kindly, quiet. Theresa buzzing like a bee, slicing tomatoes, onions, cucumbers, shelling hard-boiled eggs, opening a can of salmon, setting lunch out on the table in the kitchen. They never went anywhere, not even to a movie. Never. Except to visit family. That's it. How, my mother would later muse, can anyone be that narrow?

Her older sister Etta married late—to Simon the barber, a recent immigrant who bet on the horses and lost money. Their apartment was even tinier than Theresa's, their building dingier. The El ran right past the bedroom window, the whole place shook; you had to stop talking when the train roared by. There were no books, no magazines, no newspapers. Maybe the racing pages for Simon. No interest in anything except keeping it all going, keeping it all clean, plenty to worry about, plenty to talk worriedly about. Money, child, husband, all causes of woe and worry.

Etta was nervous. She hovered over her only child, giving her no room to breathe. I'd go to visit, since Iris was just a year older than I was, and Etta would make us lunch and stand behind us, right behind us, and watch every bite get onto the fork and travel to our mouths. How is it? she'd ask. So how is it? Is it good? It always was. Etta was a great cook; she cooked the real Jewish food, kishka, fricassee with tiny meatballs, *lokshen* kugel. Even her scrambled eggs were fantastic. But she wouldn't leave Iris alone. Fussing, watching out, being wary.

Don't go here, don't touch that; take off that blouse, it's not ironed well enough; be careful; fix your hair; look out, don't fall. Etta was extreme, huge breasts, little bow legs, cleaning the spotless. She'd bring her homemade soup to our house in a jar. First, wax paper was screwed under the lid, then the whole thing was wrapped in newspaper with a rubber band to hold it, then in a dish towel, then put into a plastic bag, and then into a paper one. Etta was the oldest; she had come to America with her mother when she was three years old, the only one of the four born in Poland, and it was as if she had just come over, believing in the evil eye, knocking on wood, throwing salt over her shoulder, superstitiously slapping Iris across the face when she got her period for the first time.

When Etta and Theresa talked about their mother, Surah, their eyes would fill with tears and they would say she was the kindest, most generous person on earth, the very best. As I got older, I would wonder, If she was so great, why are her children so stunted, so tight, so unpleasant? Except for my mother, who read books and newspapers and laughed and was loving in a way that was not disguised and who wasn't obsessed, as her sisters were so passionately, with cleaning every speck off every burner, sucking up every particle of dust.

My mother's mother died when my brother was six months old. Yes, said my mother, she was a wonderful person. Everyone loved her, everyone came to her to talk to her, she was smart and kind and warm. You would have loved her. And so talented. She would take me down to Fifth Avenue and we'd look in the windows of the big stores and pick out something for me. She would go home and make it and it would look exactly like what was in the window. But she had her dressmaking business to run, so she gave me to my sisters to raise.

They must have resented it—after all, Etta was thirteen when I was born—and they didn't know what to do with me, so I think they were mean to me sometimes. I must have been a terrible burden to them. But we had to let Mama work.

That was the way it was. My mother looked around her and saw her brother getting beaten by her father. She saw her father smiling at compliant, attractive Theresa and ridiculing feisty, argumentative Etta, whom he teased about being ugly. Her mother, the perfect one, never intervened, yet her mother was good, her mother was a saint.

So my mother made the reasonable choice; she became a good girl. Willy took her to the movies every Saturday, and he or his friend put a hand under her skirt. She hated this, but who could she tell? He hit her, but she told herself it wasn't anything much. She didn't complain, she didn't make trouble, and her sisters resented her because she was her father's favorite, the one he was easiest on. She got to graduate from high school, wear lipstick, go to college. Her father was a "typical Victorian father," used to being obeyed. That was what she told me, that was what she believed.

And then she met my father at Adams Hats, where they were both working in the office—my father's one and only office job—and he was the bad boy to her good girl. No matter what she did or what she didn't do, it was nothing in comparison to what he did or didn't do. He was self-involved, naughty, rebellious, brazen, sarcastic, cynical, even dangerous. I think that being with him enabled my mother to feel righteous and good automatically, which was crucial to her concept of herself. It was her dream, her purpose, her ideal. Sometimes he found her a pain in the neck, a worrier, a coward, but he agreed with her that she was good. He didn't want a conniving, manipulative woman like his terrible mother and terrible sister, and he didn't marry one. He wanted a good, smart, kind, caring person, and he found that in my mother, along with passivity, timidity, and an enervated sadness.

When my brother was born, in 1947, my parents were living in an apartment in Sheepshead Bay, Brooklyn. In 1948, the year before I was born, they bought one of the thousands of postwar tract houses "out on the Island." Ours, in the town of Mineola, had two bedrooms and a small yard. My parents sold it, the only house they ever owned, when I was three. From that point on, we rented apartments, and we moved every two or three years.

Most people dreamed of owning a house in the 1950s. My parents tried it, but it didn't work for them. Possessing something as demanding as a house was not what they wanted, needed, or could manage. The stopped-up toilet, the leaky roof, the overgrown hedges, the piled-up leaves—in a house, they had to take care of these daily disasters themselves. It was too much. Renting meant freedom from worrying about more things than they were already worrying about, an advantage that vaporized the appeal of equity and investment. Who could care about owning when it was so hard just to live? Who needed another burden? At least we don't own a house, my mother would say, with total sincerity.

I stood at the picture window of the house in Mineola, watching a hurricane. I must have been about two, no older than three. Water leaked under the window frame, wetting my fingers. It was gray-dark outside, wind shifting the sheets of driving rain. A metal trash can flew into the air, sailed across the street, crashed onto a lawn. At my back was a formless space, a gray, unpeopled nothingness.

The hurricane is my first memory as a walking and talking person, the memory I always cited whenever anyone asked me what my first memory was. I'd tell about the wild, dark, and crazy storm, with big, heavy objects flying through the air; how I watched, mesmerized, terrified that a trash can would shatter the window. In college psych class we were taught that first memories contain vital clues to who we are. You remember what you remember in the same way you dream what you dream: because it has profound but hidden meaning. When I'd tell my memory, though, I'd say I think I remember it just because it was so scary. I didn't see it as symbolic.

I don't know just when I first realized: the chaotic storm is my family. Certainly it was after my father told me about being a junkie, since I couldn't have perceived the memory that way before. It was funny, in a way, to discover that my first memory was a textbook case. The fragile barrier that was protecting me was my mother, but the water, the chaos, is seeping in anyway. I fear an explosion, a total collapse of safety. Behind me, where my family should be, where the living room should be, is nothing. I am alone and scared.

When I was about ten, I asked my mother if she believed in God. We were sitting on the front porch of our house on Federspiel Street in Fort Lee. There was never any talk about God in our house; none of my grandparents had been religious, and neither were my parents. The first time I saw anyone light Sabbath candles was in the apartment of my friend Madeline, in Washington Heights. Her mother tied a scarf over her hair and stood at the table, singing prayers and touching a match to thick white candles in silver holders. She had survived the camps; she and her husband both had numbers tatooed on their arms. The practice of religion had been discarded in Poland by my grandparents in favor of socialism and the Bund. Neither of my parents had had any Jewish education, and neither did Aaron or I. This was our tradition. We felt ourselves very strongly to be Jews, but praying and God just never came up. People who believed in God, who went to synagogue or church—my parents didn't demean them, but there was a sense that they were deluded, backward, holding on to rituals that didn't really do any good in the world. I remember watching Mrs. Frankfurter light the candles—her head covered and bowed, her smooth round face glowing in the lights—hearing the Hebrew prayers tumble from her lips without a hesitation and thinking: A person who has been through what she has been through, why is she still doing this? Doesn't she see how useless it has been? I felt she must be stupid.

In Fort Lee, religion was at me every time I visited Debbie's house. Grace preceding each meal, prayers and Bible passages in the middle of dinner, prayers before bed, framed prints of Jesus' handsome, hip-ly bearded face hanging in most of the rooms of the house, church choir, Sunday school, church services, Billy Graham on television, ministers on the radio, religious shows with what Debbie called "corny, bird-chirping music." I helped Debbie study her Bible passages for Sunday school. One Saturday night we took a flashlight and a Bible to the pup tent in the woods behind her house where we were going to spend the night and nearly peed in our pants with hysteria over "Do not suffer thy foot to be moved."

I checked around in myself, but there didn't seem to be any need for God. When I conjured up what God seemed to be, nothing in me leaped up to greet it. I couldn't figure out what purpose God and all these trappings served. Would people really kill each other more if they didn't have commandments telling them not to? Would more children steal candy from the grocery store? Wasn't all this just plain wrong, with or without God?

So I finally asked my mother. There were a couple of nylon-webbing, aluminum-tubing folding chairs on the concrete-floored porch, but we didn't often sit there. The porch was the province of our downstairs neighbors. Still, every once in a while Aaron and I would sit there, leaning our feet against the black wrought-iron railing, looking out at the huge horse chestnut tree, the patched and lumpy black pavement, and the jumble of grasses and weeds across the street. It was always quiet on Federspiel Street. Seldom a car, seldom a person. When Aaron and I sat on the porch, we didn't talk much, but my mother loved to talk to me, to draw me out.

She didn't like to talk about herself; if I asked her questions, she often half-answered, stopping as if she had bitten off too large a mouthful. I can't tell you right now, she'd say; it's too long a story. Or, It's too complicated; there's too much to say. But my mother had a ready answer for this question. She was not embarrassed or unsure. I believe, she said, that God is in everyone.

I probably said, Uh-huh. I can imagine myself sitting there nodding. I remember I felt elated. I might never understand what God meant to other people, but now I understood what God *was*: that part of each person that was essentially good. We all possessed a kind of perfection even if we couldn't always find it. Within ourselves we had the capability of figuring out right and wrong and of doing right. A very economical situation, very handy. No churches, no men with beards, no crosses, no prayer books, no need to kneel at the bedside at night and repeat words that someone told you to say. You could travel light.

Looking back to my ten-year-old self on the porch, I can feel again the exhilaration that my mother's words ignited. Her words gave me hope that I had the tools to become unconfused, to understand—that there was an unconfused self, an essential me, that could be discovered.

Years later, in my room at Bennington, reeling from the recent news of my father's addiction, swamped with memories, I felt I was flipping the pages of a book that I had written unconsciously, a book that contained a story I could not yet fully read but that indeed had in it everything I needed to know. Of course I had forgotten a great deal of the past, but what I remembered was enough. A wiser self, the one that had known what was important, that had come to the fore within me on the porch that afternoon when I was ten, had preserved these things for me so that if and when I got the information I needed, I could examine them.

After I found out about my father's addiction, I still had a few months of college before graduation. I used to stand in my room and look at myself in the mirror and all kinds of images and memories would flood through my mind. I saw my father's T-shirts, with their Swiss cheese of burn holes on the front, where the ashes from his cigarettes had dropped down and burned through the fabric, and I'd cry, looking at my long brown hair, my wire-rimmed glasses. I'd cry and cry, because the holes had always puzzled me; like little worms of worry, they had burrowed into me while I folded the laundry. My brother's underwear, my underwear, my father's, my mother's, piles of white cotton and elastic on the bed, his and hers and theirs, and I would touch the burned edges and they would crisply flake off. The edges were brown, not black. The ash would hang off his cigarette while he was reading, and it would grow into the trunk of an elephant, gray and long and droopy, and finally, when it was impossibly long, it fell down and rolled silently onto his white T-shirt, scattering little red sparks that set tiny fires on his chest and on the rolls of his belly. And he sat there, seeming never to feel anything, but sometimes suddenly he'd startle with a jerk, like a person roused from sleep by a pinprick, and he'd sweep the embers from his T-shirt. Then he'd subside back into himself. I couldn't understand how he could not feel those sparks, especially since they burned through his shirt. Wouldn't I feel them? What immense powers of concentration he must have, I used to think, to be so engrossed in his book as to not feel pain. And I'd wonder, Was this a good quality or was it bad?

Standing in front of the mirror and looking at myself, I saw the T-shirt as if I were holding it up to the mirror. All his T-shirts were the same: all of them were white, with round necks and short sleeves, and all of them had holes. Had he been stoned? Is that why he didn't feel the sparks, except those that burned so hot they finally registered, got through the haze or numbness or whatever it was junkies feel, or maybe it would be better to say don't feel? Is that what being stoned on heroin was like? Had he been high at home? Where did he shoot up—in the bathroom? Neither Aaron nor I ever saw needles. Whatever the specifics, the burn holes had to do with being a junkie. I was sure of that. And I felt horror, which poured out in my tears, and I felt triumph, an almost wild joy that those holes had bothered me, that I had felt there was something wrong with them. I had noticed. And I was right.

The same kind of thing happened with the hurricane

memory. Before I had the information about my father's addiction, I believed that nothing specific was wrong. That is, things were wrong in general, but there was no specific reason for them to be wrong. The ways we were different from other people, like the books my parents read, were not bad things—they were good things, I knew that. So was it simply life itself that was so miserable? Four people so unhappy, so angry, so unable to help one another, to make anything work out, as if we had all been hit on the head, walking around stupid and enraged. Four smart people in this state. This could not be inevitable. This could not always be life. There had to be a way out. And yet there it was: this appeared to be life.

But there had been something wrong, something specific, something terrible. Life had not been "normal." All those lumps of unease that clotted my throat and at times my stomach at certain remarks—Your father is working, I starved your brother—that felt on my skin like itches that I could not scratch, these had been accurate responses to disjunctions and lapses in logic. People can know, I thought; feelings can be right.

My memories all had to be reworked. In the first flush of this process, I was deluged with them. In the years that followed, the reworking came to be more like the reworking that anyone goes through: you come to see things differently as times goes by. But in that initial period my head spun with memories. They filled my mind's eye, and at times my sighted eye as well. The life line on my hand consisted of two untouching threads. I have two lives, I thought, the one before I knew, and the one after. I was in the center of them both in those last months at Bennington, the place where the old life had ended and the new one had not yet begun. In the meantime, I was writing my senior thesis, sitting day after day at my desk, a photo of Charles Olson pinned to the wall right above my Selectric. Olson wrote: People don't change, they only stand more revealed.

I examined other memories. Two very early ones had always puzzled me. In both of them, my immediate surroundings were ordinary, everyday. In neither of them was any dramatic or unusual activity happening near me or to me. Yet in both memories I felt deeply afraid. The memories were of an internal landscape of fear set in an external world of safety. The fear was highlighted by its contrast to the mundane, nonthreatening surroundings.

It was a spring morning, raining hard, and I was sitting in the backseat of a car while we waited for the next child in the nursery school carpool to come out of his house. Through the wet window, against the no-color sky, the colors of the little suburban world appeared hypersaturated: the gray-green pines, the dark paving stones, a glistening concrete jockey in a red jacket holding a lamp at the foot of the driveway, the bright, new grass. There were other children in the car. Someone else's mother was behind the wheel; my mother didn't drive. I watched the windshield wipers push the heavy silvery streams of water back and forth across the glass while unhappiness washed over me in wave after wave after wave. Unhappiness, isolation, desolation, and a sinking, sickening fear, though not of the car or the people in it. Fear and sadness swallowed me; I disappeared into them as I simultaneously disappeared into the water on the glass, the luminous, clear cascade that was more beautiful than anything I had ever seen. It was as if I were inside a crystal, with everything brilliant, sharp, and clear. I felt the essence of life, of my life but also of all life: this terrible dread and despair and the wondrous world, where there are such things as silver water and the pure, sharp smell of wet earth and cold air. There was nothing else to me—that was life, that was all there was.

In the other memory I am in nursery school, lying on the floor with my blanket during rest, looking out at the other small, blanketed figures arrayed on the polished wood. I am afraid. Not of the school, not of where I am. This is the fear that became, or perhaps already was, a more or less permanent sensation: a stiffness, sometimes to the point of achiness, in my arms and legs, a sinking feeling in my stomach's deepest pit, and a tightening of my throat.

When either of these memories came to mind, I used to wonder what had caused those moments of apparently random fear. Had it generated spontaneously? Now, in my sunny, white-walled, fern-filled college room, with my new knowledge about my father, I saw for the first time that the fear belonged to the rest of my life, that I must have brought the fear from home.

When I returned to Bennington that spring, I told my friends about the addiction. The only adult I told was the school psychologist, whom by then I had been seeing weekly for over a year. It didn't occur to me that my teachers, who had always been puzzled by my silence in class, by my embarrassed awkwardness with them, might have realized the importance of this news and would have felt, knowing it, that they understood me better. I looked to my friends for support, but they, who had always listened so earnestly to me, seemed not to hear what I was saying.

I wanted to tell them everything, to reconstruct my memories out loud, with them. Ann's brown eyes looked frightened. She bent her neck; her thick straight hair curtained her face; her shoulders stiffened. They listened in silence, gave little response. What was wrong? Couldn't they see how important this was? Then I realized they were scared, though I couldn't understand why. Why should they be distressed? I was talking about my life, not theirs; they had nothing to be ashamed of, nothing to be frightened of. The words *heroin addict* seemed to bite into their flesh and sting. They still loved me, I felt that, but I learned to be quiet; I respun the memories alone.

That spring, I thought over my life. I thought about Queens, where we moved when I was three and which we left when I was five. We lived in a two-bedroom apartment in a new two-story, boxy, brick, unadorned garden-apartment complex, woods behind, a playground in the center. There were children everywhere, swinging, running, jumping rope, drawing hopscotch boxes, walking puppies, like a Brueghel painting circa 1953.

What I remembered most vividly from the two years in Queens were scenes with Aaron. The pulling up of my underpants, my mother waiting patiently for Aaron to say, Come in. Sitting on the closed toilet seat while Aaron and his friend Dee Dee held me down and pushed a big new bar of white soap into my mouth. It was hard to breathe, my mouth was stretched, they were laughing, the soap had a horrible taste. A brown, lace-up Oxford aimed at my head shattering the glass of the living room window; it sailed in an arc, like slow motion through the air, as my mother at that moment came up the walk, and the shoe landed on the cement right at her feet. She looked at the shoe, then up at the window, then back at the shoe, puzzled, and Aaron whispered fiercely, Don't tell her I was throwing it at you.

My problems with Aaron—how he hit me and scared me, how angry he was and how bad he felt—I saw, that spring for the first time, as an integral part of our family life. Before, it seemed to have had nothing to do with anything; it appeared to have arisen, like so many of our extreme emotions and behaviors, out of air. It was now a piece of the puzzle, a part of the pattern.

I understood now that my mother had taken care of us with almost no help from my father, and that she had been dealing with the worry of his addiction at the same time. For the first time, I felt sympathy with her sadness. Things had seemed too hard for her because they had been harder than I knew. I thought about my mother's friend Merlene, an ex-Rockette, in whose tap-dancing school I had taken classes. Now I suddenly had to take in that Merlene's musician-husband had been a junkie, a "bad" junkie, my mother said, and that Allison, their younger daughter, was now an addict and that she and her big sister, Dee Dee, the one who pushed the soap into my mouth, must have had just as terrible a time as Aaron and I had.

Everything made me cry. I thought about my beagle puppy, Jingles, who died when he was less than a year old. I missed his smart sad eyes for years, the slippery feel of his loose skin against his skull, the way he licked my hand when I had a fever and sat at the side of the bed, waiting for me to get better. I knew that this was the missing any child would have felt, losing a dog. I cried now because my mother, who must have hated taking care of a puppy in addition to two small children, had gotten the dog. She had been trying to make us feel better. It all seemed so sad.

A few years before, my mother told me that when we lived in Queens she used to hear the man in the next apartment beating his wife at night. I now imagined my mother as she must have been, sitting in the living room after putting Aaron and me to bed, not knowing where my father was, unable to read or watch television, picturing him slumped over, dead in an alley, needle in his arm, or driving into a wall, nodding out. Then there is a thud next door and she listens. What can she do about my father, about herself, about the woman next door? Whatever she thinks of seems to be impossible, wrong, or dangerous. She cannot get up, she cannot move. She listens, she twists her hands, she cries.

Most complicated were my memories of Washington Heights. A few months after I had started kindergarten in Queens, we moved to this neighborhood in upper Manhattan and lived there until I was nine. My mother said we were leaving Queens to have more space, an explanation that didn't satisfy me, that sat inside me like a scream I couldn't let out, even though the new apartment did have high ceilings and big rooms. The problem was, the apartment was evil. Why were we moving to a place that was evil? The day we went to see it, I stood at the beginning of the long, windowless tunnel of a hallway that ran its length, and I knew I hated it.

It was on the second floor of 452 Fort Washington Avenue, between 180th and 181st Streets, a few blocks north of the George Washington Bridge, one of many ponderous prewar apartment buildings that lined broad Fort Washington Avenue like blocks of stone. It was not a wealthy neighborhood; the decaying brownstones and small tenements on the side streets were filled with recent immigrants, mainly from Puerto Rico. The gloomy apartment buildings on Fort Washington Avenue were home to nurses from nearby Columbia-Presbyterian Medical Center, to Holocaust survivors with their American-born children, and to white-collar workers looking for large apartments with low rent.

In our solid building what could break did. The elevator often didn't work, which didn't matter to us, since we had only one flight to walk up. One day there would be no hot water, another day no heat; everyone banged on the pipes in fury at the landlady, who lived alone on the sixth floor. In order to warm us a little, my mother lit the gas oven and left its door open. She put our underpants on the back of a chair in front of the oven so that when we put them on, they would warm up our freezing backsides.

All the walls in the building were olive green, a color Mrs. Haberman must have gotten a deal on. Vomit green, Aaron and I called it. Our apartment was repainted before we moved in, as required in the lease. White, my parents had specified, but when the moving van arrived, all the walls were spanking new, depressing Haberman green.

The doors to the street were glass and wrought iron. It took all my strength to pull one open and slip into the vestibule before the door closed on me. Walking across the stained, ice-cold marble floor of the big, dark, echoing lobby was like crossing a frozen lake at dusk. Flame-shaped bulbs burned in sconces, but too few to light up that vast cave more than dimly. A few wrought-iron chairs and couches were stranded against the walls, and at the distant end of the lobby was the mailbox room and an elevator and a double set of marble stairs, so far from the front door that they were almost invisible in the gloom. It was hard to see, going upstairs, even in the middle of the day.

In our apartment the rooms opened off one side of the terrible, long dark hallway. First came Aaron's big room, with the Ping-Pong table; then the tiled bathroom; then the kitchen, with a dumbwaiter and a wooden clothes-drying rack that raised on a pulley to the ceiling; then the octagonal dining room, where my parents slept. All the windows of these rooms looked out on the brick wall of the building next door. My room and the living room, at the end of the hallway, faced Fort Washington Avenue. They were the only rooms that had sunshine and a view and the sounds of the street: car chains jingling in the snow like sleigh bells, ambulance sirens, buses, horns, laughter, shouting, the swish of metal roller-skate wheels.

The apartment wasn't neutral space; it was alive, it had power. Ants lived in the grout between the bathtub and the tile wall; they crawled around the tub edge. Something less tangible lived in the air and turned our lives black and dangerous. The building belonged to it. It thrived in the darkness and the ugliness of the lobby, the hallway, the rooms. The light from the window in my room staved it off during the day, but at night it took over, and its presence turned all of us into our worst selves. We had no choice; the air had extra molecules in it. It was heavy to walk through, poisonous to breathe. Living was an effort.

At six I played with paper dolls, cutting out dresses, hats, and bouquets, bending tabs over paper shoulders, around paper waists. I kept my dolls in the special paper-doll folders you could buy at the five-and-ten-cent store. Each folder was made of three sections, so it could stand up like a triptych, and was fitted with rows of horizontal pockets into which you slipped your dolls. One night I had a dream that I was as tiny as a paper doll and trapped like a doll in a slot in one of those folders. All around me were other people, also tiny and unable to get out of their slots. We were all watching a witch who was stirring a big steaming pot, a witch just like in a fairy tale, dressed in black and hideous to look at and gigantic because she was the size of a regular person, compared to us. And we were terrified because the witch was eating us; we were watching as she lifted us out one by one and cooked us in the pot and ate us. People were screaming, No, no! as she plucked them out like delicious morsels, and I kept quiet so as not to be noticed, hoping that she would not see me, hoping that she would satisfy her appetite before she got to me. But then her cold eye found me and her huge fingers were coming closer and closer. Just before she touched me I woke up, and I was shaking, more scared in the dream than I ever had been in my life, and so then I knew that things could get worse than they already were.

When I finished second grade, my mother went to work for the summer as a receptionist at Columbia-Presbyterian Medical Center. Aaron was going to sleep-away camp. You will be going to a day camp in New Jersey, my mother told me. Please, no, I begged. You have to go, I'm sorry. I have to go to work; we need the money, she said. She put me on the bus every morning, though she said it broke her heart to do so. She knew I hated camp; she knew she was hurting me. She looked up from the curb; I saw her through the bus window every morning, waving good-bye, her face so sad.

I could manage at school, but not at camp. I was awkward at sports. I didn't know anything about my body, about making it run, jump, and splash. I was afraid of my body, and camp was all about bodies. At camp my mind wasn't needed and so could not help me. At camp I was a body undefended, alone. I began to fall apart.

The sun was bright, everyone was laughing, eating pistachio ice cream cones at picnic tables, but the milk in the containers tasted funny, the ice cream was green like throw-up, and the baseball game terrified me. Where should I stand, what should I do? The swimming instructor said, Jump! and we were supposed to leap off the dock, but I could do that no more than I could do any of the sports. My body would not obey the instructions. It hid itself behind bushes and crouched there, plucking at leaves and grass. My brain said, You must learn to swim, you need to learn to swim. Since my body would not obey the swimming instructor, my brain took my body down to the lake when everyone else was at crafts and told my body to learn to float. My body listened to my brain, so it tried and tried and finally one day it could float, and then one day it could swim. My brain wanted the certificate, so on the last day it made my body take the swimming test and my body passed it.

Sometimes the counselors came looking for me, but I ran away. Mostly they left me alone. Somehow they knew not to touch me, that it was better to leave me alone, not to ask me to tell them why I went away, not to try to make me stay. I knew I was not working properly, and I needed to work properly. It was crucial that I manage well in the outside world, since that world was my escape from fear, a better place than the apartment. But at camp I did not excel as I did at school. At camp I did not even blend in. At camp I failed and, in failing, I was losing the world. When fall finally came, I gripped onto the handrail of school and pulled myself up and in. I had come dangerously close to the edge, but I was all right.

I was all right, but barely. Certain things gave me great pleasure. I discovered that, under some chipped paint, the bathroom windowsill was marble, and spent hours meticulously scraping the green enamel off the sill and off glass doorknobs and glass door panels. I worshiped the mica chips that sparkled like fairy dust in the sidewalk outside the First National City Bank, on Broadway. I was mesmerized by the picture-book churchyard behind an iron fence on the corner of 181st Street, its graceful trees and green lawn a vision of peace. A soothing calm fell over me as I watched the big beautiful cone of string twirl smoothly round and round on its stand when our lemon meringue pie was tied in its box at Cushman's bakery.

At night, however, the apartment's demons swarmed through the air. I was tacked down in my bed by terror. At night it was not my room. At night the demons owned it, they owned me.

Eventually fire came to own me. My fear of fire began one night when my parents were going out, which they didn't do together very often. When they did, they usually went to Birdland, the midtown jazz club. My mother, all dressed up with heels and rhinestone clip-on earrings and makeup, leaned the kitchen broom against the wall that separated our hallway from the one parallel in Lil's apartment next door. Knock on the wall with the broom handle if you need help, my mother told me. Knock and Lil will come over; she'll be listening. I told her you and Aaron will be alone.

I begged my mother not to go. I'm sorry, she said, but parents have to go out sometimes. I could feel her sympathy, and I saw by the light in her eyes that she was flattered that I wanted her to stay so much that I was pleading and crying. To her, my crying meant that I loved her and couldn't bear to be separated from her, not even for a night.

I was crying because I was afraid of Aaron. He would come after me as soon as she left. I knew she knew he would, but she said nothing about it. This was her way of telling me that dealing with Aaron was my problem. I understood her silence as clearly as if she had spoken. There was nothing for me to say. She, who loved me, knew what was going to happen as soon as she walked out the door. By leaving me alone with Aaron, my mother was making a statement: Aaron's hitting me did not qualify as an emergency. If it did, she wouldn't be allowing us to stay by ourselves. She was telling me that I could not ask for protection from Aaron, that his punches and kicks did not merit a knock with the broomstick, leaning mutely against the wall. What do we need the broom for, anyway? I asked. Oh, my mother replied, what if there is a fire, for instance.

As soon as she said those words, fire lit up my brain. I was afraid of my brother but I was not supposed to be afraid of him, so I made fire the object of my fear. From that moment on, I began to build a case for the rationality of my fear. For example, the door to our apartment was metal; it was called a fire door. On the door was a large white sticker that said, KEEP DOOR CLOSED IN CASE OF FIRE. My mother, the door, the sign all announced that fire was a realistic possibility. Days later, my fear was fueled by a television drama about an old woman who had lost her parents and her sister in a fire when she was a little girl. Now, living in a nursing home, she couldn't sleep; she lay awake in case of fire. Sure enough, one night she smelled smoke, sounded the alarm, and saved everyone.

My brain understood this show to mean that it must not let

me sleep. My brain kept me awake so I could guard myself, so I could live. Unlike the old woman, however, my focus was on saving only myself. The fire escape was right outside my bedroom window. If I stayed awake, I would be able to escape from the apartment. I worried a great deal about the jump from the bottom of the fire-escape ladder to the sidewalk. It was a long drop. No one had told me that the ladder was made to lower automatically when there was weight on it. Still, I reasoned, I would probably survive the fall. The most important thing was to stay awake. No matter how tired I was, I must not fall asleep.

Every night in bed I listened for the crackling; I sniffed for the smoke. But that wasn't all. I saw monsters in the air, crouching, crawling. I covered my head. The street had its own demons, the gang everyone talked about, the Baldies, who particularly liked little girls with long hair, girls like me, and cut them up, played tick-tack-toe on their cheeks with switchblades. They would pull me into an alley on my way home from school and slice my face with their sharp, terrible knives.

At night I filled up with fear like an electric liquid running through my veins. It tingled under my scalp, it pressed against the tips of my toes, it filled my eyes. I had a night-light, a bulb that screwed into a battered aluminum cone that I took into bed with me so that I could read books. As long as the light was on, the monsters in the air were kept at bay. But the metal of the cone got very hot; if I fell asleep with it on, it might start a fire in the bed. I also had my dolls and my stuffed animals, especially my little horse, to help me out. I held on to them and cried, and the liquid of fear fell on their faces.

Lying in bed at night, I figured out that parents do not love their children. If they loved them, they would not have them. I would never have a child; I would never make another person go through childhood.

I knew my mother could not help me. She was always sad and exhausted. I could not tell her how I felt; it would only make her sadder. Finally, though, I did tell her that whenever I got up at night to pee, Patchy, our cat, lay in wait for me outside the bathroom door, at the end of the long dark hallway. No matter how silently I walked, he leaped out, eyes blazing, fur on end, coming at me in springing leaps, sending me running back to my room in terror, bladder bursting. Sometimes I wound up peeing in my bed. Hearing this, my mother put a battered saucepan under my bed for me to pee in. The *fendel*, Yiddish for pot, she called it. She said, kindly, The cat won't hurt you. He is just playing a game. I knew she was right. There was nothing in our apartment to be afraid of, so I knew I was a coward, and I knew I had to get control of my fears.

We lived according to certain irrational rules, carrying out decisions we did not make, as if we were obliged, under some sort of threat, to continue life as we lived it, as though we had no choice.

My father lived at the apartment, but he was not around very much. Working, my mother said. My father seemed to work more than anyone else's father, but we never had any money, which puzzled me in a subterranean way. Some people, my mother explained to me, say they don't have any money, but in fact they have a savings account that they just don't want to touch. Then there are those like us, who have just enough to pay the rent and buy food. But no matter what, unless things were absolutely desperate, my mother said, she would never save money by feeding Aaron and me hot dogs and peanut butter, as some mothers did. She poured us orange juice in the morning and cooked pot roast and made soup full of chicken feet and barley. I didn't know what it was like to want for good food, but I lusted for *things*. I wore my cousins' hand-me-downs, but I had my eye on a white fake-fur jacket in the window of the department store on Broadway. I pined for it. I wanted a doll with closing eyelids from the doll hospital. I felt I would die of longing for it. A hard-hearted beast reared up inside me when I spotted something I wanted, and I begged and pleaded ruthlessly, knowing that my mother, wanting me to feel better, might give in. If she did, if I got what I wanted, I was much more glad than guilty. I treated my perfect objects and my beautiful pieces of clothing with scrupulous care. I knew very well that buying me the mouse-gray suede penny loafers I coveted meant that someone else in the house had to do without some necessity, but that awareness didn't diminish the joy I felt as I watched my shoes hit the pavement on Fort Washington Avenue on my way to school.

My father bought a hi-fi, new records; I recall him breezing in and out, while my mother alone was responsible for us, and the effort required was just barely within her grasp. She pushed her body along, putting one foot ahead of the other, just making it to the grocery store or the laundry room. Sometimes she screamed and yelled. Once, raging, she picked up the cat and threw him against the hallway wall. The cat yowled, and I froze into a column of horror because I knew this cruelty did not exist within my mother, but yet there it was, she was being mean to the cat, and it was as if the world had ended.

According to our unspoken rules, I had to be sacrificed to my brother because he was sick, and this sacrifice would help appease him, would make him feel loved. This arrangement could be made because I had extra of everything. Extra brains, extra good looks, extra good personality, extra affection from my mother. I had in abundance what my brother did not have enough of. My brother was a mismatched piece of luggage, even monogrammed with the wrong initial (he got *A* and we all had *S*). He didn't belong, and we had to make that up to him.

My mother felt sorry for me, but she had to follow the rules; she had to let Aaron do as he wished with me. It was impossible for her to intervene. She was simply a bystander. She cared about me but was unable to change anything, as if she were forbidden.

My two jobs, being hit by my brother and listening to my mother, being her friend, required skill. The more I distanced myself from the pain of Aaron's fists, the more of it I was able to stand. The more I cheered my mother up, the better I felt. I had the satisfaction of a job well done.

But the fear was always there, shimmering and iridescent. Fear stayed with me from then on. When I was an adult, it became fear that there was someone in the house, someone who would kill me.

Sitting that spring in the upholstered Victorian rocking armchair in my room at Bennington, looking out the window at the mountains through a haze of cigarette smoke, I thought about the apartment in Washington Heights. I was still afraid of it. I thought, I wouldn't go inside it again. I wouldn't take the risk, even though I knew now that it had no power, that it was only an apartment, even though I knew now that the fear had not come from the air and out of the walls but from us. Even knowing this, I wouldn't go back inside that apartment, not for anything.

I left Washington Heights racked with anxiety and insomnia and phobias (umbrellas, escalators), but in Fort Lee I became, gradually, a child. I was a child for nearly three years, from age nine to almost twelve, when we left the brick house on Federspiel Street two months after I started sixth grade.

We were kicked out of the apartment on Federspiel Street after my father, at the height of his amphetamine use, had a fight with our landlord, something about paint drips on the washing machine. There had even been blows, I gathered, or threats of blows. The landlord said we had to get out in two weeks. My parents hastily found an apartment in Englewood Cliffs, the next town north of Fort Lee, and called the movers. For the fourth time in my life, all our things were packed; somehow in this move, my precious shoebox of arrowheads and Indian beads and clay pipes was to disappear, never to turn up.

The night before the movers arrived, I fled the house and lay among the rough weedy grasses in the dark across the street and gripped the stalks and sobbed. I loved this place, these few streets, this bit of earth, the ramshackle houses, the tilted fences, the magnolia tree in the woods. It felt like home, and I couldn't believe that we were leaving. I would lose the woods and Debbie. Everyone reminded me that I could come back to visit, but it would not be the same, I knew that.

My parents had rented an apartment on Irving Avenue, in the "bad" part of town. Englewood Cliffs had two distinct sections that even geographically didn't touch. Our neighborhood had originally been part of Coytesville, most of which had been incorporated into Fort Lee some time ago. A few of these streets of 1920s brown-shingled two-family houses had for some reason been parceled off to Englewood Cliffs, which was only formally a town. It had no stores, no municipal buildings, no library, no high school, no Main Street. Mostly it consisted of a housing development that began a mile or two away from the old section of town and was separated from it by scrubby woods and auto dealerships along Route 9. The development was a stage-set universe of fancy houses with chandeliers in marble entrance halls, driveways with highly waxed, pricey cars, immature trees along the winding labyrinth of streets. The lawns had sprinkler systems, the living rooms were decorated by interior designers, and the towels in the bathrooms were color coordinated.

Our neighborhood was blue-collar: firefighters, police officers, construction workers. My family belonged there no more than we would have belonged in the fancy part of town. My parents never got to know anyone. They kept to themselves; the few adult visitors we had were relatives or musicians from New York. I had one or two friends in our part of town, but my best friends were the rich girls, the ones with the sleek hairdos and expensive kilts and country-club memberships. They didn't like coming to my house. My mother began working full-time as a file clerk at Prentice-Hall, within walking distance of our apartment. No one made beds or washed dishes while I was at school. No one was waiting with a snack when I brought home a friend. The stale air of the empty apartment, the messy rooms, shocked my friends, none of whom had working mothers— shocked them so much that eventually one of them confessed her discomfort. So I socialized in bedrooms with matching curtains and spreads and upholstered chairs looking just like the showrooms at Bloomingdale's.

I understood. Our second-floor apartment was small and ugly. My parents put their bed on the enclosed but unheated front porch so that Aaron and I could have separate rooms. I discovered snot-specked copies of *Fanny Hill* and *My Secret Life* stashed in the bureau drawers on the porch. My father's, I could tell. He blew his nose on his fingers when he read. I'd take my snack of a bowl of applesauce out onto the porch and pore over these books on my parents' rumpled bed, listening for footsteps. I didn't want anyone to find me with them. I was so turned on that I felt sleazy, as I did with my brother.

Everything was depressing. In the kitchen was an ancient hot water heater. If you wanted to take a bath, you turned a valve and lit the gas jet with a match, standing back as far as you could as the jet exploded loudly into blue flame. You had to wait half an hour at least for the water to heat up. If you left the water heater on for too long, it would blow up. When I woke up in the middle of the night, I automatically went into the kitchen to check if the heater was off. I worried about it constantly.

My bedroom window was a narrow-driveway's width away from the window of a couple whose screaming, cursing, alcoholic fights often ended with the arrival of the police. Sometimes he slashed her with the point of a bottle opener. Sometimes she went after him. It was impossible to sleep when they were going at it. In the summer, with the window open, it sounded as if they were yelling right next to my bed. I'd get Aaron, and we would crouch down below the window, peeking over the sill at the couple, watching their lighted window like a scary show on TV.

Things were badly frayed in Englewood Cliffs. Perhaps they were not really worse than they had been in Fort Lee, but there I had been distracted by the pleasures of life in the doll-house and the woods and by my friendship with Debbie. In Englewood Cliffs all the edges were rubbed raw; life seemed hopeless. My brother and I had our sexual relationship in Englewood Cliffs. My father was still shooting heroin. My mother was overwhelmed by holding a job and trying to keep house, even in a minimal way. When she came home and looked at the dishes piled up in the sink and the laundry waiting to be done, any energy she had when she walked in the door was drained right out of her. She said she didn't want Aaron and me to have to clean and cook; she never demanded that we do those things in any consistent way. You'll have plenty of years to vacuum and dust, she would say. Why do it when you are a child? One night my mother woke me up from sleep. Get up, she shouted, and put your dirty clothes in the hamper. I can't stand this! she cried. In the morning she apologized to me, miserable that she had been so distraught as to wake me. I hated that she apologized, as much as or more than I hated her for yelling, for waking me up, for being at her wit's end. It was impossible to feel sorrier for anyone else than we each felt for ourselves.

When I was about thirteen, just after I had said no to Aaron about sex, my cousin Ronnie came to live in our apartment. He slept on the couch in the living room. He was in college, so he must have been nineteen or twenty. He was Willy's son and had been living at home, commuting to Hofstra. My mother told me that Willy and Ronnie were not getting along, but I didn't know the details. Then, suddenly, Ronnie came to live at our house. He had an incredibly square jaw and exaggerated features. His body was hard; he lifted weights. His dream was to become a Green Beret. He drew obsessive, detailed, heavily inked picture of eagles with lightning bolts cracking in the background.

He had to come here, my mother said. He's worried about

himself. The other night he was baby-sitting for a little girl and he suddenly felt the urge to go upstairs and hurt her. It scared him terribly.

Great, I said. What if he starts to feel that way about me?

Don't worry, my mother said. I won't ever leave you alone in the house with him.

Ronnie lived with us for about a year. Shortly after he arrived, I overheard him tell my mother I was spoiled, and I ran up to him and yelled at him that he didn't know anything about me. In the evenings he would go into the kitchen with my mother and they would close the door and talk. I lost my mother to Ronnie and his big problems. But once he moved in, Aaron left me alone. That was good. Ronnie and Aaron spent a lot of time in Aaron's room with the door shut. I lost Aaron to him, too, but at least in part this loss was a relief.

One day I watched Ronnie chop wood. We were at our little cottage on the lake. He chopped for hours, each stroke violent. I imagined that he imagined he was chopping up people. I never got to like him. His laugh was loud, harsh. It started and stopped abruptly. He held himself stiffly, had little of interest to say. Finally he got into the army, was accepted for the Green Berets, and left us. He broke his ankle in a parachute landing and finished his stint on a base in Germany. I was spitefully glad his dream had been foiled.

All in all, it was a bleak time. Our life looked and felt threadbare, worn out, as if it was going to come apart completely. No one had any energy left to care about anything; we were all just slogging along, day to day, all of us drained. It didn't help that my friends had everything, though after an initial bout of jealousy, I discovered that the materialism of life in the rich part of town didn't really appeal to me. I envied the expensive clothing of my friends, but not their showy furniture. I wanted a rambling old house with a big porch and window boxes of red geraniums. If I had lived in a town of wealthy people who owned houses like that, I probably would have died of jealousy.

I daydreamed about going to boarding school, which I had read about in books. One day I visited the private Dwight Morrow School in Englewood, where one of my friends had transferred, and laid my eyes for the first time on the daughters of privilege and old money. If only I could be transformed into one of these casually confident girls! I would have sharp elbows and bony knees, wear an old Shetland sweater and a swinging, knife-pleated skirt, and be taught by bright, dedicated teachers in high-ceilinged rooms with rain beating against large, clean windows.

School bored me to the edge of madness. The hands of the clock stuck to the numbers like glue. But I took pride in my A's. When another parent bragged that her Sally got all A's, my mother never said, Well, so did Susan. She told me people shouldn't boast about their children. I didn't understand. It was just facts. Her silence made it seem as if I hadn't gotten A's, which was not true.

The older I got, the angrier I grew. Adults were the targets of my rage. Around them I was confused and easily humiliated and angered. Mothers looked at me suspiciously. Some of them told their daughters I was a bad influence. In junior high school I listened to Bob Dylan records; I criticized adults with no mercy, I saw no reason to pretend to be respectful of boring teachers, silly mothers, or stiff, dull fathers. And yet when adults criticized me, I was shattered. I once knocked over a lamp at my friend Leslie's fancy house. Her mother cried out,

Oh, you broke it, and I ran out of the house, seething with anger and sobbing with shame, hating Leslie's mother for not soothing me, for not telling me it was just fine, don't worry, accidents happen. How awful it was to sit with a friend and her mother in a shiny kitchen or a paneled rec room and see that familiar film of confusion and fear cover the mother's eyes. I hated that look, but I didn't know how to avoid it, and I longed, simply longed, for someone's mother to like me.

During an eighth-grade play rehearsal, I noodled on the piano while the teacher tried to talk. My punishment was to write an essay on why I shouldn't play the piano during rehearsal. The gist of my response, passed in the next day, was that since I didn't know how to play the piano, it couldn't be said that I had been doing so. Handing it back to me in the hallway between classes, my English teacher said, It's very funny, but you'll have to write it again, more seriously. I was crushed and furious. She reached out her hand, brushing my hair from my eyes, as if she were my mother and I were her daughter. As soon as she touched me, I slapped her hand away, hard. I braced myself for the lecture, the punishment, but she said nothing, she simply turned and walked away. You hit a teacher, you hit Mrs. Chenoweth, I told myself, horrified, standing in the echoey hallway, surrounded by girls who looked at me with what I felt: shock, amazement, incomprehension.

When my father went out at night, my mother, with a gripping urgency that traveled through the closed door of my room, begged him to stay home. Her words were those of someone begging, but her tone was angry and desperate. Don't go, Sidney, as if she was warning him. I'd hear his footsteps going down the stairs; he was headed for New York. She was trying to keep him from something, that much was clear, but what?

He was just going to a club to hear some music, that's what he said. What could be wrong with that? I considered the possibility that he was having an affair. It was all I could come up with, but I felt in my gut that this was the wrong answer.

I was ashamed of our messy, depressing apartment, and I hated our messy, depressing lives. But I was proud that my parents read serious books and saw the world in terms broader than their own status and security. Especially my father. He and my mother were never part of a "set" who discussed politics and ideas, the latest writers. No, everything my father passionately read and talked about he pursued on his own, sustained solely by his own interest.

Cecil Roth wrote: "A book was not to him [a Jew] as to his neighbor an object of veneration, of mystery, of distrust. It was a sheer necessity of everyday life." My father wasn't out to impress others with his knowledge; after all, he had no one to talk to but my mother and me.

He was demanding, obnoxious; he insisted that we listen to long passages from his latest literary passion. He was a regular at the library. He went through a Rebecca West phase when we lived in Englewood Cliffs. He'd barge into my room with *Black Lamb, Grey Falcon* open in his hand. His eyes were burning with excitement: Hey! Listen to this, was on his lips. I knew vaguely that there had to be people out there who read books like these, but I had never met any of them. I was used to my father's intellectual concerns being singular. In Englewood Cliffs, the blue-collar parents didn't read and the rich parents read best-sellers. My friend Leslie's father, who considered himself an educated man, was a devotee of Ayn Rand, whose works, I knew, were pseudointellectual junk. No one knew what my father read, and there was no way anyone would know. Aaron either didn't notice or didn't care, I didn't know which. Probably he felt the loss of a father as a father much more acutely than I did. He needed someone to teach him how to get along, someone to encourage him, someone who could just plain love him. That was not my father. Aaron and my father didn't share interests, so they scarcely shared anything. I had my mother's devotion, but Aaron made her nervous. My father admired my opinions; Aaron was left out of this, too.

I had complicated feelings about my father's black-humored cynicism. Life, through his eyes, was a nutty spectacle. Nothing was sacred. Icons of the 1950s and early 1960s fell before his wry commentary. He had, as they might say, no respect. When I listen to Lenny Bruce's records, I hear my father. Is there any way to say how completely and utterly out of the ordinary this attitude was in suburban New Jersey at that time? Cynthia Ozick wrote that "a cynic is acutely alert to an element of strangeness in the way matters fall out. From the Olympian's view, everything is strange—love, hate, religion, skepticism, exaltation, apathy, domesticity, class, greed, infatuation, mercilessness, godliness." This was my father's view of life. Life was weird, life was weirdness. Not bad, not good. Strange.

Once he described to me with delight an apartment in Harlem he had visited. Now I know he was probably there to score or shoot up. It was a long railroad flat. To get to the last room, you had to go through all the other rooms. Each was a different world. In one, a young girl was brushing her hair; in the next a family was eating dinner; in the next a man was playing his saxophone; in the next an old woman was knitting a sock, etc. Everyone doing his or her thing. Together but separate. Everything ordinary yet everything, by virtue of juxtaposition, odd.

I was fed cynicism all along, in jokes, in sarcasm. The day JFK was assassinated, I got a dose so big I was changed forever.

I was a freshman in Fort Lee High, in gym class, when the word came. We all went to the locker room, listening to instructions over the loudspeaker, changed out of our blue cotton gym suits with their puffy, elasticized legs, and wandered through the halls to our lockers. People were crying. Some girls had tears running silently down their cheeks; others were sobbing as they unpacked their books, shut the metal door, and spun the lock. How could this happen? This is a tragedy, I'm scared—that's what you heard. Even the boys were quiet. No kidding, no sarcasm: real fear, real shock. The whole world was crying. I walked down Palisade Avenue toward home. Everything was quiet; the cars swishing past me in the underpass sounded sad, eerie. Footsteps echoed. People in the 7-Eleven had tight, somber faces. Across the street was a small church. I went in, stood in the darkness of the back, and cried. The world was fragile, breakable, tearful. The sorrow at the heart of everything was out in the open. The whole world was as sad, as scared, as I.

I went around to the back door of our house, up the wooden stairs, into the kitchen. No one was home. I luxuriated in the feeling that the entire world was sharing an emotion, as if we were all one self, singing one note. The solemn, reverent unity made me move slowly, quietly, not to break the spell. Then I heard my parents on the stairs; my father must have stopped at Prentice-Hall to pick up my mother from work. They were laughing when they came into the kitchen, talking loud, as if it were just some normal day. Don't you know what happened? I asked. I figured they must not have heard. Oh, about Kennedy, my father said, as if it had almost slipped his mind. Then he looked at me seriously. He was just another corrupt bastard like the rest of them, he said.

The kitchen fell away and I was standing under a spotlight. Beneath its harsh glare I saw the tears of the people on the street, of the boys and girls at school, and I saw myself, standing in the back of the church, crying, praying. We were sheep, bawling because everyone else was, broken up because a handsome man we knew very little about was dead. We were fools. I knew something no one else knew, that this guy who died was no angel. My father hadn't wished for his death and did not condone his killing, but he was not going to be dragged along into some kind of mass hero worship. And now I couldn't be, not anymore. I was sad for the next few days, even for the next few years, that I had not been able to remain part of that big sadness, except for those few hours alone after school. The TV was on in our living room sometimes during the next few days, the screen a chiaroscuro of pale faces and black dresses and black suits and black horses and the black draped coffin. My eyes were dry. It wasn't that I didn't care that Kennedy was dead; it was just that now I was on the outside, looking in.

IV

It was the day after the night my father and I had dinner under the Orson Welles and he let slip, on purpose or by accident, his secret. We had just come back from Boston. My mother and I were sitting in the living room. I was on the sofa, my mother in the chair that had been her mother's chair. Upholstered only on the seat and the back, it was a chair in which you had to sit upright; but my mother, trained by her father, always sat up straight.

My father was on the other side of the wall, in the bedroom behind a closed door. I heard the TV drone through the wall. I felt a bit insane and dangerous and stepping-off-a-cliff, but I had to say: Mom, I think Dad told me last night he used to be a heroin addict.

She cried out, almost screaming, He told you, he finally told you. Thank God, he told you at last! She pressed her open hands against her cheeks and rocked her head from side to side.

The lenses of her glasses glinted wildly, and the room we were in face-to-face seemed to fall away from the rest of the world. We hung there suspended—where were we going to land?

I thought he would never tell you. I'm so glad he did! She sobbed and laughed all at once, relief and pain tangled, the release of tremendous pressure, the sound of a person at the end of a long, terrible journey, who had arrived at a place she thought she might never reach.

When I asked her why she hadn't told me before, she had an answer that was not an answer.

I don't know, she said. Maybe I should have. Maybe I should have told you and Aaron long ago, but I thought you were too little to understand when you were children. But maybe I was wrong, even then.

And this answer that was not really an answer enraged me then and every time since that I have thought of it. How stupid and blind it was of her not to see how important this was, how essential, and how passive she was, how muddled, despite being so smart, so stupidly smart.

Then it was time for the story of what really happened. The story of our lives. The story that only she or my father could tell, because they were the only people who knew the story. The story I didn't know that I didn't know.

My father had his own version, his own life in that story. My mother had hers. I had mine, lived unwittingly, and Aaron had his, too.

I listened, grafting my own memories to her story like pruned branches to a trunk. Her words poured over me, wrapped around me, squeezed me breathless. The secret caged in her was out, loose in the ordinary, blank slate of our living room.

I had never suspected. The story she told me changed every-thing. All my mental constructs were revealed as invalid or half-baked or just plain false. Everything I ever knew was sud-denly a false impression, no good, not complete. I felt, literally, that I had fallen apart. It hit me physically. Inside, I was blown to bits, and the same old body I had always had couldn't stop shivering on the sofa.

And meanwhile, impossible to help, really, was the process of reordering, reconstruction, which began the moment my mother started to speak, the instant I found out that what I had heard the night before was true. The suddenly discon-nected moments of memory could not sustain their chaos. I felt them inside my brain, seeking like iron filings the magnets of new information, frantically re-sorting themselves back into meaning, into whole scenes, into narrative and sense.

My mother didn't go into a great deal of detail, but she told me the essentials. My father became an addict when she was pregnant with Aaron. All through her pregnancy she was afraid he would die of an overdose. On the day Aaron was born, Sidney wasn't there. He was out of it somewhere, and she was alone. My mother knew nothing about babies and nothing about drugs, and suddenly drugs and babies were her whole world. She was so nervous, she couldn't think, she said, alone in their little apartment in Sheepshead Bay with baby Aaron, try-ing to take care of him, trying to be a good mother. It was hard, she said. He cried all the time, cried until her ears could hear nothing but the crying and the ringing of the phone, which she was afraid to hear, since it might be the call telling her that her husband was dead. Up and down, up and down she walked, jiggling the baby, trying to soothe him, waiting for the phone to ring, waiting for the door to open and my father to walk in, arms full of holes, veins full of junk, head full of bebop and Harlem.

My mother sat with a wailing baby on her lap, nervously thumbing through the baby advice book, searching for answers and permission. She wanted to feed him, but every time she read the book, it said the same thing: maintain the schedule, no matter what. When she painted this picture for me over the years, there had always been something wrong with it. There in the living room that afternoon I could swallow the story, now filled out by her for the first time with *terrified*s and *alone*s and the reasons for these words. Now it was not just her and the baby; now it was the whole situation that was desperate, askew, and unnourishing, and I saw how *starved* had come to be her word for what happened. She was starving in the apartment. I could see her as a real person and I could see the baby as real, the two of them starving together, afraid and alone. And it was all right; it was terribly sad, but it made sense, and I could take it in.

I pictured her and baby Aaron in that apartment in Sheepshead Bay I had never seen, and, knowing her as I did, I felt her panic, her desolation, but also her desperate, lifesaving need to do the right thing, if only she could decide what it was. Not knowing, she thought it best to follow the rules, find her way out of the twisted jungle by means of a straight path. But the baby kept crying, and the right thing came to seem wrong, stingy, mean, and cold, and that was not the right way for a mother to be, at least not the mother she wanted to be. She had stumbled into this jungle on the arm of the man she loved, the man with whom she had had the only really good time in her life, the man who made her laugh, who had been such fun. They had been like two kids, she always said, living in the

Village, leading a bohemian kind of life, going to lectures at the New School, going out to hear music at night. There had been all kinds of crazy people, nutty parties, foreign movies, nothing to prepare her for the choices to come. Now she was lost; she didn't know how to live in the jungle or how to find her way out.

She told me stories of overdoses. How my father had once been dropped off in an emergency room, left there alone, because the others in the car were junkies, musicians, afraid of arrest. She had hatred in her voice when she talked about them, and I didn't understand. What else could they have done? I wondered, but didn't ask. What did I know of the etiquette of heroin addiction? I was ignorant, just as I had been ignorant about the two spoons and the two forks set at my white-tablecloth dinner place my first night at college, even to the point of not knowing whether the duplication was simply an error. I was just as out of my league in the mores of drug addiction; I felt the enormity of how much I didn't know.

My mother told me it was an overdose that had nearly killed him that time I had to take the Phoebe Snow to Hoboken, not diet pills and alcohol, as she had told me at the time. That explained why my father had been hospitalized in Harlem. He had been found passed out in his car. A story he once told me flashed through my mind. When he was a little boy in Harlem, where he lived, where many poor Jews lived then, a man had been sitting motionless for hours in the driver's seat of a parked car. Hey, mister, someone finally said to him. Hey, mister, wake up. But the man didn't answer, so someone opened the door and the man fell dead onto the sidewalk, where my wide-eyed father stood watching. The man had been shot. Murder Incorporated, everyone said.

My mother told me that, when we lived in Mineola—from the time I was born until I was three—she sometimes went in the car with my father to his job, poking and prodding him from the passenger seat to keep him alert behind the wheel, to keep his eyes on the road, so that he could get to the store and trim the window and earn some money and not kill anyone because he was nodding out on the highway. She was so devastated talking about this, so overwhelmed with distress, that her voice broke into gasps and sobs, then pushed onward for a few more words. I thought she might not be able to keep talking. I didn't ask anything, but I had many questions. What did she do with Aaron and me those mornings? Did she leave us with the neighbors next door? How did she get home? Did she take the bus? Did she have to change buses? Did it take her hours? Did she take the train?

Her pain from back then brought up front, into the here and now, was a pain so terrible it was awesome. And it was horrible, too, to see myself and Aaron as children in the scenes she described.

After Aaron was born, she had an abortion, because she could see this was going to be the story, that Sidney was going to be an addict, that that was not going to change. So she had no choice when she got pregnant; how could she have more children with a husband who was an addict? She said she had to go to a horrible place, a horrible room. And in my mother's face and voice I saw the dark, dirty, secret room, where she didn't know whether she would live or die, but it was worth it not to have another baby, which was more than she could handle.

Then she got pregnant with me. I was an accident, and she was going to have another abortion, but one morning she woke up and knew she wanted this baby. She said to herself, The hell with it, this baby is special, this baby is mine, this baby will be for me. It was a crazy thing to do, she said, but she was sure of herself, sure she wanted me. And I was so different from Aaron, she said, so contented and cheerful, never crying, that I made her happy.

Remembering me back then, my mother smiled. You were the most wonderful child, she said, full of little songs and stories, always talking to yourself, humming and singing. You were like a ray of sunshine in the house.

I must have looked skeptical. Really you were, she insisted.

She told me that during the time we lived in Washington Heights, after one of my father's overdoses, people from Child Welfare, or whatever it was called in those days, came to our apartment.

They wanted to see if I was using, she said. To see if they should take you and Aaron away, put you in foster homes. But when they met me, they could see right away that I wasn't like that. They could see that I was taking good care of you two. So they let you stay.

I said, Those years in Washington Heights were so terrible.

Yes, they were, my mother said. Things got so bad that I finally had to sell your father's life insurance policy to pay the rent.

She struggled to control her voice, not to sob out, as she recalled her desperation, forced to shed the only financial security we had. However meager that security was, she knew that at any moment we might urgently need it, since every time my father put that needle into his arm, he was at greater risk of death than the average man. She must have felt, after she sold the insurance, that if he died we would be lost, dropped into bottomless poverty, with no foothold to help us climb out.

As she spoke, my memory drew forth from its dim recesses the policy itself, a set of crinkly, crackly, heavy pages folded in three. On the front was fancy writing in blackest ink. The policy, along with a few other important papers, was kept in a small black metal box with a lock, in the top drawer of my parents' dresser. The lock was never fastened, and I sometimes took out the documents to feel their serious, unusual heft, messages from the outside, grown-up world, like artifacts from another planet. Also in that dresser, right in the same drawer, was another artifact, equally formal and mysterious: my grandmother Surah's evening bag of cool and sparkling jet beads that glinted in my hand like stars in the sky.

Did you know, my mother asked me, that I slept with a butcher knife under my pillow when we lived there?

No, I didn't, I replied, aghast. Why?

In the silence between us, her words sounded like the ticks of a clock in an empty room.

She said, I was afraid that someone would break into the apartment through that fire door in Aaron's room, the one that opened out onto the fire escape. Remember we couldn't lock that door? It wasn't allowed by the fire regulations. Sidney was never home, and I had to protect us, somehow.

I didn't know my mother had also been afraid. But her fear had been contagious and I had been infected. It hadn't come sui generis from me. She had lain alone, night after night, in the double bed in the room that was supposed to have been the dining room, listening. Under the pillow that was under her cheek there had been a blade sharpened to slice, even to kill. Her fingers had clutched its handle at a creak of the boards. Meanwhile, in my narrow bed, I was listening for the crackle of flames, each of us protecting the other, who, we believed, was sleeping soundly, safely, unafraid. How ironic. And no wonder I hadn't been able to tell my mother my fears.

One of the hardest things, she said, was how isolated she felt. Her mother was dead, her father was no help, she had no friends on whom she could depend. She was all alone with her burden. No one understood anything about heroin in those days. Not how to get off it, not how to help the addict. It was horrible, she said. It was a nightmare.

Did you ever think of leaving? I asked.

She shook her head at this question, so easy to ask, so hard to answer. Oh, I thought about it, believe me I did, I thought about it all the time, she said. But where would I have gone? What would I have done? No one in my family could have taken us in, even if I had wanted to live with them, which I didn't. None of them had the money or the room for us. And if I was out all day working when you and Aaron were little, who would have taken care of you? Some stranger? You couldn't stand it when I left you alone even for a minute. You would beg me not to go out, plead with me, hang on to me, grab my clothes. So I felt I couldn't leave you, I couldn't do that to you.

Did you know, she asked, that Aaron went to a therapist for a while when we lived in Washington Heights? The therapist was always trying to get me to come and see her, to talk to her, but I never did because I would have had to leave you alone in the waiting room. I knew you would have been so upset.

I shook my head. I had known none of this. I knew that Aaron went to see a woman who helped him with his reading, but I had no idea she was a therapist. I remembered that Aaron at least once went to see her by himself, that my mother and I watched from our living room window as his small, hard, determined body crossed Fort Washington Avenue and waited at the bus stop. The bus came, blocking him from our eyes, and when it went away, he was gone. He couldn't have been older than nine or ten, but in those days little kids often went around New York by themselves. Aaron and I used to take the AA local one stop to school together, even when I was in kindergarten and he was in second grade, and we'd stand with our noses to the window of the front car, our hands pressed to the glass to keep ourselves from falling over.

This woman had wanted to help us, and my mother had refused. She had been presented with a chance to get help, and she hadn't taken it. She blamed it on me, and she blamed it on her good mothering. She believed she had protected me because she didn't sit me down in the waiting room with crayons and paper and walk away. Maybe I would have been desperate if she had. But that hadn't been the real reason. She hadn't wanted to go into the room, close the door, sit across from the woman, answer questions, cry, think, talk, decide. That was obvious, whether she knew it or not. After all, she did leave me alone at times, she did go to Birdland, however reluctantly, and she did sometimes go next door. If she wanted help, if she really wanted it, she would not have allowed the short-term kindness of not leaving me in the waiting room to win out over the long-term issue of leaving us all where we were, leaving herself hiding behind my fear.

My mother said, Anyway, if I had kicked your father out, how would I have managed? There was no welfare in those days. Or maybe there was something like it, but it never occurred to me that there was, or at least it didn't occur to me that it could be for me. There was such a stigma attached to it, you just didn't think of it. It was something for the lowest of the low, the absolutely desperate; it was so shameful.

And besides, how could I have left Sidney? What would he have done without us? He would have had no reason to go on. I'm sure he would have died. I used to picture that, me leaving him and then him dying. I would have felt I killed him. I would have had that hanging over me for the rest of my life, as if I had murdered him. I couldn't live with that. And he was my best friend. How could I leave him alone?

I was appalled. The way she felt—that she could get no help, that she was alone, that there was nothing better, that there was only something worse—I knew I must have that inside me, too, that giving up, not being able to cope. Would I have acted differently from the way she had? Would I fall apart as I got older, if trouble beset me the way it had beset her? I didn't want what happened to her to happen to me: I didn't want ever to be hopeless.

And what about Aaron and me? Didn't she know that we had been the true prisoners, the ones who really had no choice? I resented that we had been kept ignorant of the facts of our lives, that she had turned our welfare into a reason not to leave my father, rather than a reason to go. Who knows what would have happened to us if she had kicked him out? He might have died, he might have lived. We might have suffered more, we might have flourished. At least, she would have acted. For her, staying with him had been playing it safe. That, to my mind, was an unbalanced equation.

Did he ever try to stop? I asked. I knew nothing, and I could see that my ignorance exhausted her. She explained hurriedly. To her it was an old story.

Everyone, she said, tried different things. Some people even went to clinics in Europe, where supposedly there was some kind of cure, but nothing worked. Your father went to several psychiatrists over the years, but he only respected one of them. You know how he is. He had no patience with the Freudian stuff.

But there was this one doctor your father actually liked. One day that psychiatrist called me up on the phone. He asked me about my life, about you and Aaron. He said that I had to either shit or get off the pot. I was shocked at his language. No one talked that way then if you didn't know the person well, especially not doctors. He said I had to figure out a way to support you children so that if Sidney couldn't kick his habit, we could survive without him. He told me that things could not, should not, go on the way they were.

The psychiatrist, a genius, a man far ahead of his time, it now seems to me, had listened to my mother's concerns and worries. How would she manage? We can make a plan, he said. So there, on the phone, they did.

We were living in Queens at the time. The plan they made was that my mother would find a large, cheap apartment in Manhattan, with enough bedrooms so that she could rent out a room to a boarder if she had to. In order to get my father to agree to move, she would tell him that we needed more space and that she wanted to be in the city so that he would not have to drive so far to get home at night; that would give him less time to be a danger behind the wheel. Once we moved in, she would issue the ultimatum agreed on with the psychiatrist: either kick the habit or get out. If he didn't quit, she would throw him out and find a boarder. The income from the rented room would mean she would not have to work full-time, that she could still be home when Aaron and I came back from school.

My mother had completed two years of college. When she

worked the summer she sent me to day camp, she had, without any trouble, gotten a job as a receptionist at the Columbia-Presbyterian Medical Center. She had proved to be a good, hard worker outside the home. In the mid-1950s there were jobs for women as intelligent as she was. It would have been possible to carry out the psychiatrist's plan.

I never understood why we moved there, I said. I told her I was amazed to find out that there really had been a reason, that I always felt we had been drawn there, like zombies, led to the terrible apartment by some secret power. The psychiatrist had been that power.

Yes, said my mother, that was it.

So what happened? I asked. Did you tell Dad he'd have to leave if he didn't quit?

Yes.

Well, did he quit?

My mother laughed. No, he didn't quit. And I didn't throw him out. How could I?

I felt sick with grief and frustration. For this we had moved to Washington Heights? For this nothing outcome? My mother, the good girl, had obeyed the authority, the doctor. She followed through with the plan until the crucial moment, and then gave up. Had she ever intended to go through with it? Had she ever even asked herself if she would? Had she grilled herself, really given herself the third degree? Had she made herself any promises? No, most likely she had just stumbled along, as usual, knowing that what the doctor told her was a good idea, a wise idea, the best idea, and so she followed through, without being ready, as they say, to go all the way. If only she had known that she would never kick him out. Then we wouldn't have moved to that place where the outside world was as frightening as the world behind the apartment door. There would have been no gangs of bright-eyed teenage boys, no old men in hallways sticking their hands under felt circle skirts, no gobs of spit on handrails up dark, dingy stairways.

Moving to Washington Heights had turned what was already a bad dream into a nightmare. Malignant dust darkened our windows into perpetual twilight, leaching colors of their hues. At the worst of times a dense fog had billowed through our rooms, wrapping us in a suffocating blackness that pressed on us like the weightier atmosphere of another planet, making it hard to move. If one lay down, it was hard to get up.

My father walked into the living room. The air was so charged with the past that his corporeal reality was discordant, shocking; he had been our subject and now he was standing barefoot in front of us, a middle-aged man in chinos and a white undershirt with no holes. He had given up cigarettes years before, when the information on lung cancer came out. No problem, he just stopped, instantly and easily disposing of that addiction and never looking back. He stood glancing from me to my mother. We were red-eyed, shaken, obviously distraught.

Did he know what we had been talking about? Had he been listening to the sound of our voices over the sound of the TV, waiting for our conversation to wind down so that he could come in and stand before us, the tale telling and the crying mostly done? Did he wonder what we had said while he was in the other room?

You told her, Sidney, my mother said. Instantly his defensive wall shot up; so he did know what we had been talking about. He turned to me, angry. What the hell do you care! he shouted. It was years ago, you were a little girl. It was my life, not yours. What the hell difference does it make to you?

His eyes, blazing. His voice, fed up with us. We were bugging him. He didn't sit down; he was just visiting.

I was so used to the structure of the drama that I didn't question its necessity: my mother and I talking, my father and brother either absent or off to the side. Never all of us together.

My father stood there wrapped in a kind of impenetrable, maddening innocence, the same innocence that always enfolded him. The innocence of isolation. I felt shamed, humiliated, as though I had been caught doing something wrong. I didn't fault my father for listening through the wall or walking in on us coldly, his eyes accusing. I felt shame because we had been talking about him behind his back. What I didn't see was that he had turned his back, forcing us to talk behind it if we were going to talk at all.

Abruptly, he went back into the bedroom. What about Aaron? I realized that he didn't know and that neither of my parents had said, Let's tell Aaron, we have to tell Aaron. Neither one had mentioned his name. No one talked to him, no one ever talked to him.

I was always the one who got the news. This particular news was different from and far more important than any I had ever before received. It was not fair to keep Aaron from knowing it one moment longer, to leave him one more instant in ignorance, befuddlement, outside the truth. I was falling apart and re-forming second by second, and I knew that every second counted. Every second that he didn't know what I knew was robbing him of a second of his life, his real life.

Someone has to tell Aaron, I said, but my mother, for whom

there had been no secret, said, No, I can't, I'm too exhausted, too upset to do it now.

She got up and went into the bedroom. When would she tell him? She might put it off and off and off. I sat down on the red-patterned rug, with the phone in my hand, and dialed Aaron's number. He was living on Sixth Avenue, right on the corner of 14th Street, in a loft over what had been, when he moved in, a Blarney Stone, a cheap corned beef and cabbage cafeteria. Then a souvlaki joint opened up under him. The loft reeked of grilling meat, even first thing in the morning. Across Sixth Avenue was an office building. When you got up in the morning and walked to the windows, you could see people in suits and dresses filing and typing. If they looked across the avenue, they could see you in your bathrobe looking at them, sipping a mug of tea.

I heard the phone ringing in the loft. When he answered, I found myself saying eagerly, Aaron, guess what, you'll never guess. Suddenly I was excited, as if I were about to reveal to him a delightful surprise. The truth was a treasure, a priceless wonder that I could give to him. Aaron, I said, did you know that Dad was a junkie until you were fifteen?

Then all at once my face was burning hot. Maybe he knew. Maybe he had known all along but just hadn't told me. Maybe he would say to me, I knew that, you asshole. Maybe he would tell me I was a jerk for making such a big deal out of something that was no news to him, something he just took in stride.

At first he was silent. Then he said, I'm going to come out there to kill that fucker. I'm going to tear him apart. I'm going to kill him.

He was serious. Don't come, I said, stay where you are. I began to blab, throwing facts my mother had told me at him through the receiver. I told him I wanted him to know everything I knew. If I filled his head full of information, the world would crash down on him as it had on me and he would be pinned beneath it. He wouldn't be able to make it out of his chair, much less down to the subway and across the river to New Jersey.

Then he cried on the phone, and I felt I was swimming, nothing solid to hang on to except the tiny, precious island formed by the shattering news.

Bennington was still a women's college when I arrived there in 1967, but at the end of my sophomore year, the student body of 350 voted to make the school coed. Shortly after the vote, feminist consciousness hit the campus in a big way, just as it was hitting the rest of the country. Suddenly everyone was reading feminist books and passionately reevaluating history, love, friendship, art, marriage, sexuality, ambition, and even our college in that light. By the middle of the following year, feminism had dramatically altered our sense of ourselves as women. We looked around us with new eyes: we saw what somehow we (unbelievably, it seemed) hadn't seen before: we were a women's college with a history of male presidents and mostly male faculty. We didn't need more men, we needed fewer. But it was too late; we had to live with the consequences of our vote. During my junior year the first male students arrived, most of them transfers from other colleges. One or two of them in a class dominated the discussions. Few of us knew how to assert ourselves or were even sure how we felt about being assertive. We talked a great deal about our mothers, about the limitations of their lives, about the messages of self-effacement we had received (don't argue, don't make trouble, don't shout, etc.).

During the spring of my senior year, my thoughts ran often to my mother, whose "true story" I had only just heard. On the one hand, she had done nothing "wrong." She had been faithful to her husband through thick and thin, she had not abandoned her children, and she had never put herself first. Aaron and I had ungratefully nicknamed her "The Martyr" long ago. Perhaps there was a TV show she wanted to watch; she immediately relinquished her choice if one of us had another request. If there was soup only for two, she offered it to us. She demanded almost nothing for herself and even then always seemed to feel she hadn't done enough. I had to admit to myself that, given our family situation, I was lucky she had been that way. If she had been selfish and preoccupied with her own concerns, what would have become of Aaron and me? On the other hand, if she had been stronger, she might have left my father.

The whole idea of action fascinated me. I pondered the Yeats line: In dreams begin responsibilities. This was a wholly new way of thinking for me. Life had been something that happened to us, something far stronger than we were. When I was little, I was terrified of tidal waves. I sat in the sand and imagined one rising up, a huge wall of water towering over Jones Beach. I feared I would look up and there it would be, filling the sky, the end of us. That was what life was, a terrible, unpredictable, powerful force. My mother worried but did not act, out of fear of making things worse, out of fear of asserting herself. My father acted but didn't worry, didn't take responsibility. I had no idea of what it might be like for an adult to be in control, relatively speaking, of his or her life.

My mother was a sympathetic person, a feeling person, a frightened person, a caring person. In many ways she was the "good person" she wanted to be. But she had not left my father, she had not protected me from Aaron, she had not fought for Aaron in school. If you are not part of the solution, you are part of the problem, went the 1960s slogan. I am not a doormat, I am not a chair, my mother used to shout at my father in frustrated rage. She had not been happily passive, stupidly inert, but tormentedly paralyzed.

All it would take to make me cry was to remember her saying that afternoon: I slept with a butcher knife under my pillow every night when we lived in Washington Heights.

I saw the apartment. It was dark. I was lying in my bed, on alert, sniffing for smoke, my seven-year-old body aching with tension and exhaustion. My mother was lying awake in the double bed in the dining room, her hand resting on the wooden handle of the knife. She was listening for footsteps, floorboard creaks, cries for help from Aaron, whom the intruder would encounter first.

She was afraid, and she was waiting. She lived like a coward and yet within that life she was brave. She never set goals, made plans, but she put a knife under her pillow to defend us.

When I was a little girl, the first time I heard my mother on the telephone canceling an appointment with the excuse that my brother was ill, I was shocked. When I asked why she had lied, she said, Oh, it doesn't matter, what's the difference? I began to notice that she embellished these white lies a little more than necessary, filling in such details as what one of us had come down with or making up a story about having to see her sister in the hospital, that sort of thing. The lies she told were always small and harmless, but they unsettled me deeply. I could never get used to them. I got the idea that part of her enjoyed this pretending, as if she had a secret room of eccentricity, piled with a jumble of masks and many-colored costumes. I sensed that that room was secret even to her, with only a few silly, errant lies allowed to escape, like smoke slipping out from under the door.

That afternoon in March I found out that there had been many large lies told to protect, shield, preserve, avoid. The lies had been so dense around us that I couldn't see them. They were so tangled and twined around one another that they could not simply be hacked down. They would have to be unwound, little by little. That afternoon and the months following were the beginning of years of undoing mats and twists, painstaking, delicate work in which the metaphor was obvious: replanting, revealing, growing, digging, emerging, unearthing.

I was cynical, bitter. She had lied to us long after she needed to, long after my father had stopped shooting up, long after we had grown up and were gone from the house. I thought, sardonically, she did a good job of lying. She didn't think she was good at much, but she was good at that.

When I heard her tell those little lies on the telephone, it was as if the floor beneath me had fallen away. But now I saw that the floor had been a fabricated one, made up for Aaron and me. It was not the same floor my parents walked on. No wonder it was easy to fall through.

All my mother's reasons for not leaving my father seemed to me, that spring, to be doorless walls she had built to justify keeping herself from acting. It wasn't that I knew that staying with my father had been the wrong choice, or even that I believed there could be a right or wrong choice in such a situation. What disturbed me, thinking over what she had said, was the degree of her pessimism. Her negative assumptions—that if she left him he would die, that she would not be able to support us, that she would not be able to find a good baby-sitter for us—

had all made it impossible for her to make changes. Because she was faced with such beliefs, leaving him had not been a viable option.

The American ideals of taking control of your life, setting goals and working toward them, were not rejected by my parents; such striving was simply not within their reality. My father's musician friends seemed to have been born playing great; I never heard about or saw them learning or practicing. I thought people who achieved remarkable things did so without effort. Picasso painted great right off, Brando acted great from the first. Talent was all. If you had to work at something, it meant you would never really be that good at it, so you might as well not try. Did my parents tell me these things? I never saw either of them work at something, learn a new skill. It was just not what they did. They admired greatness, certain sorts of achievements; they were in awe of the miracle of a written book, a painted picture. But it went without saying that those who created these wonders were just not like us.

I finished my senior thesis that spring by taking amphetamines and pulling all-nighters. I felt so smart, so capable, when I was speeding. I could figure anything out. At dawn Ann and I would stagger out, laughing and barefoot, onto the wet grass and smell the country smells and listen to the birds and watch the mist lift. Our heads ached, our bodies ached, our brains were frying, but in our rooms were my brilliant pages on Charles Olson's poems and Ann's brilliant translations from ancient Greek. This stuff is too tempting, we said to each other. It's dangerous; once this is over, we'll never take it again. And the truth is, we never did.

I didn't know what to do with my life after graduation. I could go and live in New York, find a job, but my brother was there and my parents. It was unbearable for me to talk to my parents now. I was furious at my father. He wouldn't say he was sorry; he wouldn't ask how it had been for me then or how it was now. He was defensive, annoyed. No reason for such a fuss, he said. Screw you all. Leave me alone. My mother looked at me beseechingly, which inflamed my anger. What did she want from me? When Ann said, Let's move to England in the fall, I said, Okay.

A couple of months ago, I packed up a tape recorder and walked the few blocks up Massachusetts Avenue from my house to my mother's apartment. I had asked her if I could talk to her again about her marriage and my childhood, and she had agreed. Twenty-five years had passed since that conversation in the living room, and although she and I had talked here and there about her early years of marriage and motherhood, I now wanted details that had been irrelevant that March afternoon. The story was now part of me. I had become integrated into it and it had become integrated into me, and what I had never thought possible, what I could never imagine, had happened. I had become detached. Now I had the luxury of curiosity. I knew I could listen to whatever my mother had to say and, however awful the details might be, not feel threatened to the core. I held no grudges; I no longer felt rage. The story was sad, but it was over. The story was me, but it was not all of me any longer. I had written about it, and I had discovered that rendering accurately what I had experienced had lifted the past onto the page and out of me. Years of therapy had helped me beyond measure. I no longer cried for the terrified girl I had been. I looked at that girl and saw instead that she had been blessed with certain equipment that she used to make the best out of her childhood, and in that way she was lucky. And lucky in so many other ways, too. Lucky to have sought and found help, lucky to have fallen in love and married a wonderful person, lucky to have been able to change enough to have children and be a decent parent. Lucky to live in a pleasant house with white curtains at the windows, and lucky not to have to worry about money in that terrible, grinding, wearing-down way that her parents had in her childhood. Lucky to know her luck, lucky to have enough.

My mother and I settled down, the recorder on the floor between us. Tell me, Mom, I said, how you first found out about Dad using heroin. Did he tell you?

Once I was pregnant, I began to find out, she said. He was using before that, but I didn't know it. You know how he loved to tell you everything that happened to him. So he told me. And I'd notice his eyes were pinpoints, so I'd know. That's when I began to shut down. It was the only way I could live. I was always walking around with this terrible feeling in my chest. I just lived from day to day. I'd take care of what I had to take care of, and then I'd plop down. It was the only soothing thing I could do.

The night I went into labor with Aaron, George Handy was over and Terry Gibbs, and they were all high as kites, and they took me to the hospital. I was ashamed all the time. I was always making excuses. Sidney visited me in the hospital and his nose would be red, and I'd say he had a cold. He'd sit in the chair and his eyes would start to close, and I'd tell him it was time for him to go home. And every time he left, I knew he was getting into the car, and so then I'd worry he would kill someone. I wasn't so much concerned about him getting killed. Not that I ever hated him; I never could. We were really very well suited. But he might kill someone else. That's what bothered me so much.

He never shot up in front of me. He'd go into the bathroom and he'd be there for a long time, and then he'd come out and say, No, I didn't do it. And I'd believe him. For a long time I believed him. He'd say, I will stop, this is it, but of course it wasn't. It was just horrible. I never knew.

You know, I said, I just read a book about Stan Getz, which I took out of the library to try to understand that whole scene, and the guy who wrote it says that after nodding out on heroin, you feel great for a while, all energized. I never knew that. I mean, the image I had is that the person is really out of it, just sitting in some corner nodding, and that's all. Reading that, I understood at last how people can use heroin and do things like play music when they are high. Or go to work, like Dad did.

My mother said, Oh yes, that's true. He'd get very clear and energetic. He'd scrub the floor, mow the lawn, do the shopping. Everyone thought I was so lucky to have a husband who washed the floor. He had so much energy. Sometimes he'd do things a little too hard, if you know what I mean. Especially for a baby. He'd pick Aaron up and carry him around on his shoulders, and I would be afraid that he wouldn't see the doorway or whatever because he was high. I was always in a state of fright.

Money was ridiculous. But I have to say, if we didn't have money to pay the rent or the heat, I'd tell him, and the next job he did, he'd give me all the money. I knew he didn't want to lose his family. He didn't say so, in so many words, but I knew it. We were terribly important to him.

The first time he went to the hospital, we lived in Sheepshead Bay. Aaron was a baby, maybe sixteen months old. I had gone over to my sister Theresa's for a few hours to stay with my father so that Theresa and Sol could go out for a walk. My father was living with them then, and he wasn't well. I left Sidney with Aaron. I still believed him when he said he wouldn't do anything. I felt pretty secure, leaving Aaron with him. Except for fire. He was always smoking in those days. Everything in our house was burned up with cigarette holes. But I felt bad for Theresa. So I put Aaron to bed and went. Anyway, Al Cohn came over and they got high and Sidney overdosed and Al left him there. I came home and there he was on the kitchen floor, making this horrible sound—he couldn't breathe. He was turning dark. I didn't know what it was. I was petrified. I called Al Epstein and he came over and threw out the works. I called a doctor—I just picked a name from the phone book—and the doctor came and I asked him not to call the police. I was standing there with Aaron in my arms; the doctor must have felt sorry for me, because he didn't call the police. But the hospital did and then the police called me. And they were nasty to me. They wanted to know if I was using drugs; they wanted to take Aaron from me. I said no, I wasn't, so they said I had to see a doctor, this young man, who said he thought Sidney should go to Rockland State Hospital, where they would do tests. Sidney's mother and sister had already been to see the doctor and they agreed with him. I said no, it would be so bad for him; he's not insane in any way. So the doctor sent him home in my care.

I was mad at Al Cohn for a very long time for that, that he left Sidney and a little baby. Sidney would have died if I hadn't come home. But I shouldn't have been mad at Al. He was nuts then himself.

The second time he kacked out was in Stan Getz's house. The Getzes were also living in Queens, I think. You used to play with Stevie, his oldest child. He was a nice boy; you two played beautifully together. Anyway, Getz and his wife brought Sidney to Queens General and left him in the emergency room. They just dumped him there. The doctors found him and didn't know what was wrong with him. They called me up and asked me if he had a medical problem. They said they didn't have much time, they had to act quickly, so if I knew anything, I should tell them. So I did.

When I was nineteen years old, I shared a house in the Berkshires with a friend for the summer. A man shone a flashlight up the dark stairway at three A.M. and creaked up the steps slowly, slowly, out there with no telephone, no neighbors, and finally he came into the bedroom and the covers were over my head but I could feel him right next to me and I could hear him breathe and hear his clothes rustle and I was waiting to be stabbed or shot or ripped apart, although *waiting* is a ridiculous word for what it was, a kind of suspension of time, reality, hope, dreams; a moment of utter everything and utter nothing, being in a bowl stirred by the spoon of fate. Swish swish, which way will it go? Death or life, hell or salvation, you name it because I could not have, at that moment, named anything, floating as I was above my life or maybe submerged below it, below or above the very realness of reality, but not in it, certainly not part of living as I had known it until that night.

Eventually the man inexplicably walked out of the room, down the stairs, and out the door. He had stood by the bedside for seconds of real time, eons of hallucinogenic terror. After he left, I gradually, little by little, hour by hour, day by day, week by week, returned to life, to college and lunch and cars and flowers and conversation, but something in me had shorted out from too much terror and I could not get unscared. The terror of those sleepless nights when I was six, seven, eight, nine reerupted. I couldn't sleep; I was afraid to be alone. I woke up automatically every night at three and listened until my ears were ready to pop, just as I had once sniffed for smoke like a bloodhound in the dark. At first I jumped at every little sound, day or night. Then only night was really hard, but that didn't go away.

When I was little, I believed that my fear came from the world, augmented by my inner weakness. There were so many things to be afraid of. There were the demons in the air at night, the fire waiting to be ignited, the gang members with their cold eyes and switchblades. I believed that I was susceptible to fear, in the same way that I was susceptible to strep. The germs were around everyone, but only certain people got sick. I had a weakness: I was frightened by things that other people took in stride. Other children knew there might be fires, but other children, I was sure, slept. I was ashamed of my weakness. And what could anyone do for me?

In my twenties, after I learned about my father's addiction, I saw my fears as a reflection of the insecurity of our lives. My mother had lived in fear: about money, about my father, about my brother, about taking care of us. No wonder I had been afraid. I had been living on quicksand; any moment we might all sink.

Aaron scared me the most. But it took me a long time to know that. I *was* susceptible to fear, our life *was* insecure, my mother *was* dependent on me, but Aaron wanted to kill me. The only way to deal with this kind of fear was to split it off.

For many years of my adult life I continued to separate what had gone on between Aaron and me into a sort of netherworld, a special zone, that I accepted as a reality but from which I drained most meaning. I would have said to you it had been something painful and terrible; equally, I would have said it had been nothing much.

I might have told you that my childhood resembled the dreams I had: someone is coming into a house to kill me. I call the police but the phone doesn't work or the person who answers laughs or puts me on hold and I am screaming, Help! into the receiver but no one will come and I will have to face this dangerous person all alone, and I know that I will not be able to protect myself. I can't think, all I can do is feel the fear, creeping along my skin and shooting up in waves inside my body, and my body knows that the only thing that will help it is not to be there, but it cannot go away.

Until I was in my mid-twenties, I would have said that all my years of fear had not damaged me too much. I might even have let you know my secret worry: that I had not had such a bad childhood, but remembered it as being bad because I was a negative and oversensitive child. If my childhood had been so terrible, wouldn't I be more messed up? Yes, I was often very unhappy and confused, but so was nearly everyone. I saw a therapist because I was determined not to live the rest of my life ruled by these muddling emotions, but I was not crippled by them.

However, when I was twenty-five and crossing Lexington Avenue, the street became unstable and wavery and I felt as if I were not in real life but in a frightening dream, watching myself move my legs down the sidewalk. I knew it wasn't a dream, it was reality, but it didn't feel real. I was terrified. This sensation hit me crossing Washington Square Park a few days later, then on 14th Street; then it began to happen everywhere, more and more often. After trips to several doctors, I learned I was having panic attacks. They seemed to have erupted out of nowhere.

I was all right in my apartment, but to get a quart of milk or a newspaper, or to hail a cab or catch a bus, I had to cross Sixth Avenue. Sixth Avenue at Charlton Street was busy, with traffic going uptown from the Holland Tunnel. Women in house-dresses sat on folding chairs in the park at the corner, watching their children play, while a few doors away cops unloaded stolen goods at the police warehouse. There was a drugstore on the other corner that sold almost nothing but had a bank of telephone booths. It was a Mafia neighborhood, very safe. But now I'd look across Sixth Avenue and it was as vast and unsteady as a sea. I would never get across. When I got to the middle of the street, the curb was still miles away. The air weighed too much. My head was too high up, my feet so far away. Sounds were hollow, ringing, too loud. Colors too garish, lights too bright. I was dissolving on the shifting, tilting, unreal earth.

Terror was everywhere. The subway was miles under-ground, the world above it unreachable; the faces were blank, frightening masks. I gripped the seats of taxis, pinched my arms, to tell myself I was real, the world was real. I knew I lived in reality, but it didn't feel real; it had the texture, light, and sound of a dream. I kept going out because to stay inside, where I was safe, was to die. I couldn't give in. I decided the attacks were messengers sent to remind me that the fear I felt all those years had not just gone away, that it was living inside me, rising up to demand attention. The fear had been terrible; it now insisted on being heard—would not allow me to push it down.

Years passed. Different theories were advanced, different remedies offered. I tried psychotherapy, hypnotherapy, Valium, behavior modification, cognitive therapy, relaxation, meditation, but the fear was far stronger than any of them. It shifted and mutated but it stuck, leaping out in the car, the supermarket. I had had enough fear early in my life, more than enough; maybe that was the problem, maybe the fear had changed my brain and my brain was never going to be able to live without its daily regimen of fear, as if panic were some sort of food it needed. And it no longer mattered how my brain got the fear; it could manufacture terror from anything. It turned the innocuous into the monstrously threatening, so that life was like a nightmare itself, with terror overwhelming me during a walk in the woods on a beautiful summer day.

I had wound up living in fear again, like a woman who was beaten by her father and grows up to marry a batterer, except that it was my own brain that had failed me, that had brought me back to this place I hated. I tried to make friends with fear; I introduced the new fear to the old, and all the steps I took helped me to understand myself, but they didn't chase away the fear.

One morning when I was living in London, a couple of years before I had my first panic attack, I woke up and for an instant was back in childhood: I relived the precise feeling, not just the memory of the feeling. And when the moment passed and I was back in the present, I knew that if I had to feel like that now, every day, I would kill myself. Because the feeling that I reexperienced was horrible, despairing terror, and it was dreadful. It was exactly how I had felt as a child and it was an ordinary feeling for me back then. I never thought of suicide as a child; all I had wanted then was for childhood to be over. I lay under the blankets in my single bed in the freezing cold bedroom of my furnished apartment in Hampstead, shaken.

The fear had been repulsively intense, even worse than I had remembered. I pushed aside the covers and stood up on the icy floor. Across the room from my bed was a mirror. I looked at myself and I looked normal, fine, a twenty-two-year-old in a flannel nightgown with hair messy from sleep, like anyone my age anywhere in the world just getting up. I did not know, absolutely did not grasp, why I had been so frightened as a child. I had all the raw information I needed to answer the question, but like Dr. Watson, I saw everything that Holmes saw—I saw the air vent, the fake bell rope, the bed nailed to the floor—but I could not make sense of it.

After the attacks began, the ante on my questions went up: Why had I been so frightened as a child? What relationship, if any, did my panic attacks have to that fear? Did they have the same root cause? If so, and if I could discover that cause, would it help the panic attacks go away?

In 1987, several years after the panic attacks started, I came across a summary of my problem in *The Diagnostic and Statistical Manual*, the offical handbook of psychiatric diagnoses. I don't know what the latest edition says, but that old one painted a picture of me. It said that panic attacks—or agoraphobia, as the disorder was most often called then—were more common in women than in men, had their onset typically in the sufferer's mid-twenties, and often occurred in women who had

had highly stressful childhoods, in which they were, as the book put it, "the parentified child." The onset, it said, often followed a significant loss.

My loss had been leaving my therapist. In London I had worked illegally for a small publisher, writing copy for art books under assumed names for nearly two years. One day a letter arrived from the office of immigration: I had been found out, and I had two weeks to leave the country. My therapist offered to contact the authorities and explain that it would be detrimental to my emotional health to stop seeing her. I misunderstood, thinking that she was offering to make this high-level intervention just to be nice, to allow me the opportunity to stay in England if I wanted to. I could not conceive of being at any real risk simply from leaving my therapist, no matter how important she was to me.

I was twenty-three and felt invincible despite chronic confusion and depression. My therapist was a light in that darkness, the only person who could show me the way I had been searching and yearning for all my life, the way out of confusion, the only adult who ever understood me, who didn't want comfort from me, who could demand hard work and excellence from me, who understood me better than I did myself. She was all that to me—no therapist could be more—and, because I had seen two therapists before her, I knew that this kind of respect and understanding is rare, but I left anyway. I missed New York, and I didn't want to become an exile. I had seen a movie in which an immigrant says living in a foreign country means you never quite "have your ass in your pants," which perfectly described how I felt in London. I had a good life and many friends, but I was never really comfortable. If I had stayed another couple of years, all my friendships and connections would have been there, and it would have been even harder to start over again in New York. I was relieved that the government was making this decision for me. My therapist looked at me with sad concern in her eyes when I told her that I didn't want her to intervene, that I was going home. No, I said, pushing her away without knowing what I was doing, as I had pushed away Mrs. Chenoweth's hand with a slap when I was fourteen.

I went back to New York and moved into my apartment on Charlton Street, which is called Prince Street on the east side of Sixth Avenue. I looked for another therapist, and I looked for a job. New York is like the Wild West, the superintendent of my building told me, meaning that the city was dangerous and lawless; but I loved it. I had always loved it, and now I loved it even more. The angles of the buildings, the sunlight on brick and on the cast-iron structures that loomed over West Broadway, the little Italian butcher on Prince Street, where short old women all in black conversed in Italian with the butchers and bought *bracciole* and where, standing next to them, I felt conspicuously tall and blond even though I am of average height and my hair is only light brown. I loved the bodegas and the steamy smells and the hollow-metal loading docks and the weird little clothing stores that were opening here and there in Soho before the area had that name. But I missed my therapist. Not a sentimental kind of missing, but a sick feeling in the chest of leaving something valuable behind. I tried seeing a man therapist, but that was a disaster. In fact, it was on the way to his office that I first had a panic attack. Although he had come highly recommended, he seemed to me supercilious and not very bright. I despised him. I hated his stupid plaid pants and white shoes. How could I respect anyone who dressed like that? I hated the cheesy modern furniture in his office. I hated the stacks of journals piled on his desk. I told him I didn't respect him; I told him I hated him. He nodded and gave me a smug little smile. Finally I quit. I knew he wasn't good for me; I knew I didn't need to hate my therapist. I needed to respect and love my therapist, and I had left behind the one that I did.

When I quit, he called me on the phone, argued with me, said he was concerned that if I left now, I might develop serious problems. I couldn't be swayed. I agreed it was revealing that everything about him threw me into a rage, but why was that therapeutic? No, I said, forget it. I will never set foot in your office again. Finally I found a woman therapist who was very nice and supportive, but she was too close to my age, too casual for me. I loved the formality of my old therapist, her brilliance and her distance. I felt safe under her assessing eye. She was smarter than I was; this new therapist was not. Still, this therapist was helpful, and I was going through a terrible time, trying to get my panic attacks under enough control to live even a crippled sort of life. I was working as a copy editor; I was in graduate school; I needed to get around the city. Taking the subway all the way uptown to City College at 138th Street was sheer torture, but I did it nearly every day.

I met Maury when I was living on Charlton Street. I had been having panic attacks for about a year, and I had lost not my love for the city but my ability to enjoy it. A walk to Bleecker Street for homemade sausage was doable but an enormous strain. It helped tremendously if a friend was with me, but even then it was hard. Maury knew about my problems, but it was as if they were some sort of light, removable wrapping around me that he could barely perceive. We completely and totally enjoyed each other. It felt, as they say in songs, as if we had come home.

We lived in Worcester, Massachusetts, for three years so that Maury could complete his residency in family practice, and there, in that boring city of steep hills, Maury taught me to drive. It snowed endlessly the second winter we lived there, and the third winter was the blizzard of '78. I began to see another therapist, the best one I could find there, a woman, again close to my age, and again there was this difficulty for me, that I felt she was too familiar, too friendly, and ultimately not sharp enough to help me sort out my story. I missed Dr. Dewar's incisive clarity as much as ever. Then, when we moved to Cambridge, I was sent, through a consultation I had set up with a well-known therapist, to a psychiatrist some years my senior. She was dignified, spoke with a British South African accent, and her office bookshelves were lined with art books as well as texts. Not only were her trappings reminiscent of Dr. Dewar's, but she listened to me with the precision that I had sorely missed. Her age, her professional distance, and the questions she asked released me. In the very first meeting with her, I cried and cried. I was not evaluating her; I was there with her, in common interest, in common cause. When I left her office that first day, I knew that now I could finally get to work again.

The panic attacks did not allow me to forget my history; that was good. My history crippled me; that was bad. Everything I did, everywhere I went, required enormous effort. Over the years the attacks waxed and waned, but they never went away. Sometimes it was a struggle to walk down the block. Some years I could drive on the highway, some years I could not.

I had not come out of my childhood unscathed, as I had once thought. My panic attacks forced me to recognize that my wound was serious. After ten years of attacks, I had to face the fact that I had a chronic condition, a mental wound that could be palliated but could not be healed. Fear still had the better of me, even though my daily life was not threatening, as it had been when I was a child. I was not afraid of what surrounded me, just as I had not been afraid of the car or the nursery school; again what I was afraid of was displaced. It was no longer fire or escalators or bugs. Now it was crowded spaces and empty spaces, big spaces and little spaces, highways and subways.

Finally, in my early thirties, I took the pieces of the puzzle that concerned Aaron and me and I began putting them together. I was married and living in Cambridge. My psychiatrist worked half the week at the local Veterans Administration hospital, treating Vietnam vets, where the new diagnosis and understanding of post-traumatic stress disorder was being explored, and she applied some of that knowledge to treating me.

One day at my weekly appointment we were talking about how I still at times woke up at three in the morning, heart pounding, listening, unable to go back to sleep. I believed that this was a memory of the man breaking into the house in Stockbridge. Here I was, so many years later, still reacting to the event in a literal way. I was frustrated, looking at my therapist across the room, sitting in her Danish-modern chair, next to the long, low table on which stood potted African violets and cyclamen and, at my end, a box of tissues. You know, she said. Her hair was pale, the color of nothing, and her eyes were pale, too. You know, no one is any longer trying to kill you, she said, and then we talked some more, about my brother; and the curtain, as it were, was lifted on the scene, and there it was, laid out before me clear as could be.

It's very exciting when you finally give yourself credence for something you should have given yourself credence for long ago, when you take a part of yourself into yourself and digest it so that now it's part of everything else that is you, not some piece of you that you observe. For me, that meant giving credence to the reality of physical pain, how much it had hurt, how it had punched holes in the space in and around me.

I began to want to be around other women who had been physically hurt as children. I needed to hear what they had been through. Although I had friends whose childhoods had been difficult in a variety of ways, it happened I did not know anyone who had been constantly hit.

I joined a twelve-session group for women survivors of sexual abuse at Massachusetts General Hospital. I wanted to find a group for women who had been battered as children, since I felt that being hit had been more damaging to me than the sexual aspects of my relationship with Aaron, but I could not find such a group. In the end, it turned out not to matter.

There were eight of us and two therapists. I was amazed that nearly half the women were Jewish, including one wife of a rabbi. I knew that their numbers reflected the tendency of Jews to turn to therapy as a way of working things out, that it was not an indication of an especially high rate of sexual abuse in Jewish families. Nevertheless, it shocked me; there is a stereotype that Jews are not physically violent, as there is a stereotype that they don't drink or become addicted to drugs.

I assumed that each of us would tell her story right away, that we would go around the circle, one gruesome tale following another. In fact, this happened, but much more slowly. It took almost the entire twelve weeks for all the stories to be told. Everyone in the group but me was having severe relationship problems. Only one other person was married; the marriage was not good and her relationship with her children was very destructive. No one had a successful career. Hearing about all this damage was depressing, more depressing than the stories themselves.

One woman's father had raped her when she was nineteen; her mother had listened to the rape from her bedroom across the hall, both doors wide open, and had done nothing. Another had been systematically tortured by her brother, who urinated on her face, tied her up, and so on. Every time someone told her story, the rest of us listened with utter sympathy and a kind of awe. How did you stand it? we'd ask, not rhetorically. We really wanted to know. My story was nothing compared to your story, we told one another, meaning it sincerely.

We told each other, You were so brave, but when the others said the same to us, we said, Oh no, I wasn't, not like you. We had minimized our own stories when they were happening, and we never stopped doing so. That's why it took me so long to give myself credence, to see what was hidden from me but in plain sight.

Aaron, who lived thousands of miles away, came to visit. We stayed up late, sitting on the couch, talking. My children were little; he was married but he and his wife had decided not to have children. He said he was amazed that I had done so. He believed that he was too damaged to be a good parent, and he was skeptical that I could be one. He spoke as though we had inherited an irreversible fatal disease. He said it seemed to him that it was safer to remain childless. I used to feel that way, I said. I never wanted to have children when I was younger, I knew I would not have been a good parent, but now things are different. I see that it is possible to take good care of children and for children to feel secure enough to suffer less than we did. I see now that our situation was extreme, not as terrible as many others, but much worse than most.

It was strange to be talking to Aaron face-to-face. For years we had barely seen each other. There were his nervous, elegant hands, his thick, golden-brown hair, the face that so many thought was handsome but that looked to me always too tight and edgy to be appealing. We talked on the telephone now and then, but Aaron was abrupt, gruff, not one for chitchat.

I had only recently spoken to my father for the first time about what had gone on between Aaron and me—all the hitting that had plagued my childhood. It was not long ago that I had stood at my kitchen window, staring blankly into the chalky white siding of the house next door, holding the receiver in my shaking hand, listening to my father say, If anything like that happened, I didn't know anything about it. Now I was talking to Aaron. We had never talked about this subject before. I had no idea what he would say.

I've been thinking a lot about what went on between us when we were kids, I said to him. You mean how I hit you all the time? he asked, without missing a beat. The alacrity of his response surprised me. It was as though he had been waiting for me to bring this up. Yes, I said, and I've been realizing how much it affected me, that it was the biggest influence on my life, really, and I've been thinking that it was probably—it had to have been—just as much of an influence on your life, if not more.

Aaron's wife came into the living room and asked, What are you two talking about? Aaron answered: About how I used to beat the shit out of my sister. His wife said, All brothers and sisters fight. And Aaron said, No, I mean I used to beat her up really badly all the time.

It seemed to me that Aaron wanted his wife to listen to him, to ask him what had happened—what he had done and when and how—but she just shrugged and said, Well, yeah. Her indifference surprised me. Maybe she cared and just wasn't the kind of person to show her concern in front of someone; maybe she would talk to him about what he had done to me when I wasn't around. I really didn't know her at all. Still, it struck me that he wanted to talk to her right then, that he wanted both of us to talk to her, to tell her what had happened, but that she didn't want to hear.

I'm still grateful to him for saying it: I used to beat the shit out of my sister.

I didn't talk to my mother about Aaron and me. What could I tell her that she didn't already know? Only about the sexual things we did; I knew she didn't suspect those, but to tell her would be nothing but cruel. Besides, I couldn't bring myself to mention those events to anyone but my therapist. Even with her it was almost impossible to speak about those weeks or months, whichever they were, and when I did try, what I said was fragmented and weak. I began to understand Aaron better; no wonder he didn't want to talk to anyone. What I felt guilty about I could not discuss, while the scenes in which I was victim I described with gusto.

This was a period of time during which I cried a great deal in pity for myself. I remember I walked through the house in the evening, vividly recalling being smothered, my arms being twisted, being kicked, punched, choked, this time reexperiencing all of it with the horror it deserved. I'd lie on the couch and sob for myself as a little girl. One day I went to the doctor, and the nurse jabbed me with the needle while drawing blood. I burst into tears and couldn't stop crying. I wanted to hit the nurse, to smash and pound her, to kill her for hurting me. I no longer could pride myself on how well I took pain; I no longer could space out and take myself away from it.

I wasn't in therapy because of the panic attacks. Even if I had never had a single attack, I still would have been afraid of my brother, angry at my father, oppressed by my mother's neediness. I still would have lacked a story that made sense to me, and I still would not have felt that I had become a person, even if to others I appeared to be one. I still would have been very insecure about my own worth. My in-laws criticized me and I was crushed; my brother barked at me on the phone and I was shaken. I had been writing all my life, but I seldom liked anything I wrote. Yet I could not stop writing. I hardly ever finished anything. I never submitted anything for publication. Very little I wrote felt like me, yet writing was the only thing I really wanted to do; it was what I had wanted to do since I was a child. I earned an MSW and worked at a child-guidance clinic. My supervisor thought I was doing an excellent job, and I knew in many ways that I was, but the work required a selflessness that I simply could not maintain. Just because you are good at something doesn't mean you have to do it, said my therapist. Finally I quit my job to write, knowing that I might never write anything good, anything that expressed what I felt.

As I gained clarity, as the pieces of my self assumed a more orderly, coherent form, as I understood my past better, I became more assertive and self-confident, less judgmental and self-doubting. I was a good parent. I loved my husband. My writing began to go well. But the panic hung on. It was like a heavy pack on my back that I had to carry everywhere, even though I no longer needed what was inside it. I could hardly walk under its weight. It was filled with old junk. But I just couldn't put it down. I would have to carry it forever, as best I could.

V

The videotape was of my father's most recent poetry reading. His friends put the reading together to honor him. Everyone who came knew that it would be his last. He sent me an invitation, a page of homemade calligraphy, swirls and scrolls. For a myriad of reasons, some of them practical, I didn't go. Now he was showing me what I had missed. He told me eagerly that he wanted me to see how many people had come, how many friends he had. There they were on the television screen, assembled on bridge chairs and easy chairs, the living room packed with them. I watched him come into the room, shaky and skinny and pale, dressed in a baggy gray sweatshirt and blue jeans, making his slow way through the crowd, raising the walker, setting it down, raising it and setting it down, greeting people as he went, a serious cast to his face. The guests grew tearful, watching him. Some of them, after he had greeted them and moved on, took out tissues and dabbed their eyes.

My father kept looking at the screen until his video image sat down in the chair that had been placed at the front of the room. Then he turned to look at me. When I didn't say anything, he spoke for me: I still can't believe it, he repeated incredulously, shaking his head slowly. They all came to see me.

The camera scanned the audience, jumping from face to face. There was Doris, my mother's childhood friend from the Bronx. And Al Epstein and Savina, his beautiful wife, once a big-band singer and still glamorous. The rest of the faces were from more recent years; most of these people were closer to my age than to my parents' age, friends from the men's and women's movements. My mother and father were the elders of the group, the parental figures, and these were their quasi-children.

I felt bereft, looking at these unfamiliar faces, many of them openly grieving the impending loss of my father. I had met a few of these people, but most of them were strangers. Where were the men and women I listened to through the wall at night, picking up the secrets of a language that my teachers and the parents of my friends did not speak? Dead, estranged, or drifted away over the years, until there was almost no one left who could be there except for Al, with his little mustache and tired eyes, and Savina, in her mink and heels, shapely legs crossed.

In 1983 I went to New York for a party to celebrate my father's self-published book of poems. Al came up to admire tiny Eleanor, pressed against my chest in her Snugli. Like most of the adults who came to our house when I was a child, Al had seemed scarcely to know I was alive. Now, staring at Eleanor, he spoke with vehemence: We never should have had children, none of us. We didn't know what we were doing; we just had kids. It was just what you did in those days; you didn't think about it. You didn't ask yourself if you were ready for them, if you wanted them, what it meant to be a parent. So of course we screwed up. We didn't know shit about ourselves, let alone our children.

My parents had friends named Frank and Joanne Sokolow. Frank was a musician. My mother was in the hospital for a hysterectomy for a week when I was in fourth grade; Joanne was at our house every day that week when Aaron and I came home from school. On one of those afternoons, she took me to Lord and Taylor in Manhattan to buy a pair of Capezio shoes I had dreamed of owning ever since I saw a drawing of them in an ad in the *New York Times*. Soft, delicate, red kid—shoes with flat heels and a strap across the instep that fastened with a mother-of-pearl button. They were even more beautiful than I had imagined. One night when Frank and Joanne were over, I was awakened by shouting in the living room. Get out of this house and don't ever come back—my father's voice quivered with fury. I heard the door open and close and footsteps going down the stairs, out onto the porch, then a car door slam and the car drive away. What happened?

Your father got mad at Joanne, said my mother in the morning. Her words were drops of water falling, falling, down into a well, never hitting bottom. Why? I don't know, she said. It's too complicated to explain. She was sad but noncommittal. That was the end of Frank and Joanne.

That's basically how it was. Friends came and went. No one stayed around except Savina and Al. There were arguments, estrangements. Years later they might be back for a while, or my father would see this or that one at clubs, but no more family visiting. There were years when hardly anyone came around. No one had paid much attention to me, but I missed them. When Al Cohn stopped coming, I missed him, missed his glass eye and his birdcalls. Zoot was my favorite, my crush. I was in love. Twinkly eyes, thick, tawny, brushed-back lion's hair, slow and easy way. He was there, then gone for years, then one day he was back. Want to come with me to pick up Zoot? my father asked. We stopped at the bridge, Zoot got in the car, just back from touring the Soviet Union with Benny Goodman. I kept looking at him from the backseat. No one I knew had been anywhere, least of all to Moscow. He asked my father to stop at a liquor store. Getting back into the car with a paper-bagged fifth, Zoot cracked, We got the booze, let's cruise. The world opened up before me, roads leading everywhere, people taking them, no stopping. Let's cruise.

All the time these guys had jokes. Biting, clever, show-biz jokes. The ones who played in pit bands for shows were fountains of jokes. I heard a million of them. And they were dry wits themselves, Zoot being among the funniest and the driest. He had his own delivery: deadpan and worldly wise. His cleverness stunned me into silence, not laughter; his spare asides left me breathless and awed. He was cool, centered, ironic, pithy.

I remember one joke. It wasn't Zoot's; I don't know who told it. Two hipsters are walking down Fifth Avenue at Christmastime, and there's a crucifix outside a church, and one of them looks up at Jesus and says, Hey, baby, why ain't you smilin'? Don't you know it's your birthday?

I was twelve years old when I heard that joke. Did I know a single person I could tell it to? Christian or Jew, it wouldn't matter; nervousness would flicker across Debbie's freckled face, Leslie's bony one. They wouldn't get it. It was a joke about hipsters, but they would think it was a joke about religion, and they would be offended, and I would never be able to explain.

On the videotape, my father was reading his poems. Suddenly he tugged at my sleeve. I wrote this one coming up for you, he said, earnestly. My heart leaped in anticipation of a poem of apology, of recognition, of understanding.

NO LO CONTENDERE

> my case is closed
> it has no appeal
> even to me
>
> marauding regrets and recriminations
> find me empty and defenseless
>
> is it any wonder
> the voice is shrill
> the protest a whimper
>
> my heart will not plead its case
> anymore just now
> or ever again

My father hadn't gotten in touch with me after getting my letter a year ago, in which I told him I needed a respite. I knew he wouldn't call or write until I told him to. It never crossed my mind that he might.

At the time, when my mother told me that my father was terribly hurt at my rejection, I felt guilty, but not guilty enough to give up a vacation from our struggles. I hated the rage that imprisoned both of us when we spoke. I hated the way he saw me and the way, when I was with him, I felt myself to be. He said I was mean and vengeful, and when he looked at me, I felt I was. He seemed never to consider my point of view, my experience of being his daughter. Was it possible that he really didn't? How could a person not look at his own role in such a standoff? Why was he so stubbornly insistent that I was the only one who needed to change? I wanted him to apologize to me, to take responsibility for his actions. He said he wanted to "forget all this father-daughter crap," wipe the slate clean and just be pals, since we had so many common interests, including my children. I was constitutionally incapable of surrendering to this demand. Every cell in my body rebelled, raged, boiled. I could have been tormented, tortured; I would never say that the past didn't matter. I knew, as surely as I knew anything, that the past could not be gotten over except by accepting its reality. I felt painfully the weakness of my personality, that I could be so tangled up, so destroyed, by his refusal to see my experience as real.

Months passed. My mother reported that my father was still deeply distressed. I asked myself if I was being monstrously cruel to him. I knew if I were a stronger person, his misconceptions would roll off my back. If I were a more solid person, his not seeing me would not make me disappear. I longed to feel my own reality so intensely that I would not need another's confirmation. I longed to be able to see my father and not be threatened to the core. Was I indeed cruel, as he said I was, as my mother seemed to agree I was, as Aaron seemed to believe I was? My father portrayed himself to my mother and brother as devastated by my rejection. My therapist sat back and said, Did he try to get in touch with you after you wrote him that letter?

Of course not, I said. Well, my therapist pointed out, a small smile on her lips, he did not have to accept your decree without a fight, you know. He could have appealed to you, he could have called, written, come to your house, insisted you talk things over. He did not have to do what you said.

Oh, I said, completely taken aback. Suddenly I saw a basic, obvious truth that had escaped me all my life, one that I hadn't even known was eluding me, one that was elementary and extremely useful and without which life was infinitely more complicated: my father was free to respond in any way at all to my letter. I may have been accurate in my prediction that he wouldn't resist, but I did not cause him not to resist: that was his own responsibility and had not been controlled by my request. And I knew that my father didn't know this; I knew that my father would say he stopped talking to me because I asked him to; I knew that my father was not aware that he acquiesced for his own reasons, not mine.

My father saw himself as rejected, victimized by me; he just as easily could have seen our respite as sensible, necessary, a time to cool off and think. Perhaps I had given him a parental role in which he finally felt comfortable. Up until now, I had blamed him; now he could feel justified in blaming me.

His brown eyes searched my face. He didn't have any idea that the poem pained me. He was simply proud of it, and he wanted me to be proud of it, too. Its content was subsumed underneath that desire. His mother may have hurt him on purpose, I really don't know, the night she made him read her will aloud. That had been a serious crime, a felony. Reading this poem to me was only a misdemeanor; I knew he was not deliberately causing me pain.

On the screen, my father picked up a sheaf of papers from

the small table that had been set up beside his chair. He introduced what he was about to read as a first attempt to write about his early life. The pages he read covered many topics quickly, as though he had written them racing against the clock. His theme was the development of his masculinity. He began: "I grew up in Brighton Beach, Brooklyn, a working-class, almost totally Jewish community in the 1930s. I learned my masculinity in the classrooms and handball courts at Abraham Lincoln High School, but especially at Chiam's poolroom, at Brighton Fifth Street."

He read about the Depression, about radicalism, in his high school. "It didn't take much to radicalize people then; having to wear a cotton raincoat in the winter took care of that." He read about the tough guys he hung out with at the poolroom, their "vacuous faces framed by their tan sharkskin suits and white-on-white roll-collar shirts with the inevitable flowered silk tie from Leighton's," about discovering jazz: "The Savoy Ballroom and Harlem drew me like a magnet. The jazz players became my heroes, and the saying that jazz is not just music but a way of life became more and more a reality for me." He went into all of these topics only briefly, in a paragraph or two, with few particulars (and no specific mention of heroin). He read about his mother: "My illiterate mother was possessed of great intelligence and boundless energy and no possible way she knew of to use them in a personal or affirmative way. Is it any wonder she became an angry and bitter human being? My mother was not one to go gently into her unhappy prison, and she made us all pay a price for her pain."

Then he read: "And now to the man who was the most distant from me and also the man I have carried in my heart all the days of my years: my father."

His voice broke, he took off his glasses, he wiped his eyes, he tried again, but he could not continue. He shakily handed the pages over to Bob, his close friend, who, in his high-pitched southern twang, so incongruous to the material, read on: "My father was concealed from me and unavailable throughout most of my life. He was alone and lonely much of his life. He buried himself under work and responsibility and was surely buried by them. When I was young and finding no sense in his life, I dismissed him as a fool. Only now do I remember the few smiles he permitted himself to give me; only now do I remember those wintry weekend afternoons when I would come home and find him sitting alone in a dark room listening to the broadcasts of the Philharmonic or the opera. Not long before he died, he had the vision to realize how important it was for him to try and tell who he really was. And in that hospital room in the brief time left him, he finally reached out to me. It's not much, but it's all we had, and I treasure it."

That's as far as he'd gotten, just these few sketchy pages, interlarded with fairly predictable comments about women's roles: "The macho ethic was most in evidence in the lives of the musicians I came to know. So many of the women who became involved with them were passed around from man to man with about the same regard as if they were a stick of grass. And even in the world of my intellectual friends, women were still at best second-class citizens. Even though those men were more sensitive and perceptive, there was no question that essentially the women were there for their benefit and use."

I wanted more. I wanted to hear about the boardwalk and his friends and his sister and what exactly his father said to him in the hospital room before he died, and what it was like in

Harlem getting drugs and what it was like in the clubs, but there was no more.

I wanted to hear more about his artist friends in Brighton Beach, his high school buddies through whom "the names of Kafka, Joyce, Auden, and Picasso became familiar and meaningful to me." I wanted everyone to know that not only was he in the poolroom on Brighton Fifth Street and in Harlem listening to jazz but also he was reading Kafka and Marx and going to the Metropolitan Museum of Art and listening to Stravinsky. I wanted them to understand how hurt he was, and yet how he was able to hang around not just with the hard guys but also with Allen Eager and Tiny Kahn and the painters Larry Rivers and Jane Freilecher and Nell Blaine. I wanted to know how the surf felt on his face, how the wood of the boardwalk felt under his bicycle tires. I wanted him to write about what his mother said to him, about her strong arms rolling out noodle dough so thin you could see through it, about him and his father arguing so bitterly over communism versus socialism that they stopped speaking for months.

The tape ended. My father clicked off the television, and I placed the remote control back on the bedside table, next to the water glass and the tissue box. For a moment we were both silent. Then he asked, Remember that program I was in up at Yale? To be part of that experiment into alternative cancer treatments, my father had had to write an essay and be interviewed. When they accepted him, he was thrilled. He soon had to drop out, however, the disease outdistancing the cure.

Well, he said, one of the things they did was they gave me a tape to listen to. They said it would help me find the little boy inside me. If I could heal that little boy, they said, maybe I could start to heal myself. At first I thought, What the hell is this? But then I thought, What do I have to lose? So I started to do what they said. I'd put the tape on in the living room by myself at night and try to concentrate on finding him. And you know something? I did. I would stay there in the living room with him like they said to do and be nice to him. It made me cry. I would sit there and cry, like a baby.

I thought of the framed photograph of him in the hallway on the bookshelf, a four-year-old in knickers, holding his big sister's hand. I studied that picture all my life.

Now I saw the little boy walking down the street alone, and the man, the grown-up of himself, coming along, taking the boy's hand, holding it tight, saying, Let me walk along with you. The people at Yale wanted to heal him of cancer, but I didn't care about that, I wasn't sorry he was dying. All I cared about was the boy and the man touching hands. The boy didn't smile back at the man; he was too unsure of himself, too unsure that this was real. The man felt the small bones under the soft skin of the little boy's hand; it was almost as if he were touching another person for the very first time.

My father asked me if I ever watched *Mr. Rogers*. Yes, I said, anyone who has children watches *Mr. Rogers*. My father's face was turned to me, his eyes were burning. I said that Eleanor and I liked *Mr. Rogers* better than *Sesame Street*.

My father would have laughed at Mr. Rogers if he had been on TV when Aaron and I were growing up. He would have deflated him for us. He would have poked fun at his midwestern drawl, his songs, his sweaters. Most of all he would have gone after his sincerity. He would have laughingly said to us that, in real life, Mr. Rogers probably hated children or loved them in some sort of twisted way. And I would have been forced to admit to myself that this might actually be true.

So I was more than a little surprised when my father got to the point. He said he had been watching *Mr. Rogers* lately. Do you know, he asked me, that he is on more than once a day? Sometimes, he said, he's on three or four times, on different channels. Yes, I said, I know.

Without mockery, my father said, He is wonderful—don't you think so?

Then all at once I understood. Yes, I think he is, I said. My father nodded. He is like the parents you and I never had, I said, and my father nodded again.

I did understand. I sometimes cried when I watched Mr. Rogers. I cried silently, and I wiped away the tears before Eleanor could see them. I thought of myself, a photograph of me, sitting on a couch in Washington Heights, my eyes unreadable. I cried watching Mr. Rogers because the girl on the couch could have been helped by his words. My father cried because he needed those words. And now, when he was just about to die, he was letting himself hear them. Mr. Rogers was being his daddy. My father searched the channels for him, and as many times a day as he could find him, he watched. He was learning. That was why he could know now that he never saw me as a person, never considered how I felt. I wished I could tell him that I loved him, I wished I could say, as Mr. Rogers does, I like you exactly the way you are.

When Maury said that my father had only a few more days to live, I decided to stay with my mother to take care of him. Maury went home to Cambridge to see his patients, and Max and Eleanor went to stay with Maury's parents in Connecticut. My mother called Aaron, and he flew to Newark Airport and joined us for three days of round-the-clock care before my father died. We took turns. One of us was always with him. He lost his ability to speak coherently a few hours after he talked to me. He went rapidly downhill. It hurt too much to talk and the increased pain and morphine allowed him only flashes of clarity.

We didn't know what we were doing. It was Christmastime and hard to get nurses and doctors on the phone to ask advice, to ask what was normal, to ask if we should give him more morphine. He begged, when he could speak, to have Maury come and kill him. He could hardly swallow. One of us sat up next to him all night in the dark, holding his hand. We couldn't tell whether he was going to die in the next minute or whether he would suffer and struggle for another day or two days or even more. We had to force the morphine pills down his throat. We drugged him up; we let him suffer; that was all we could do.

As I sat next to his bed for hours, never once did I feel, I wish he weren't dying. Never once did I feel, I will miss him. I felt only, He is dying, this is death. I felt, He is home, we are taking care of him, and that is the right thing to do.

I saw that death is a grueling but straight road. There is no turning back once you are on it. I saw that death is like childbirth, a big body struggle with no stopping, the outcome inevitable.

My job was to be with him. He could have been anyone. He was a human and I was a human, ornaments of personality and trouble rubbed out.

Once, delirious, he sat up, his legs off the side of the bed. I reached forward to steady his arms. His bobbing head on his weak neck came toward me. He bit me, hard, near my collar-bone, through my shirt. At first I didn't know what the pain was from. It was hot, searing, as if a terrible, enormous insect had stung me.

I helped him to lie back down. Clearly, he didn't know what he had done. I went into the bathroom, pushed down the neck of my T-Shirt. There were bright red teeth marks on my skin; over the next few days they bloomed greenish yellow and purple, spread like a sickly sunset.

I went to get the mail for my mother. I hadn't been outside of the apartment for two days. I took the stairs to the lobby. It was evening. The linoleum floor gleamed strangely; the low sofas and fake chinoiserie lamps and jars were dreamlike. I wasn't ready to reenter the world outside the apartment until he was dead. Walking toward me through the lobby was the singer Phoebe Snow, whose face I knew from photographs on her record jackets. I loved her voice. Al Cohn played on her first album; her stage name was the same as the name of the train that I took from Binghamton to Hoboken when my father overdosed. She was just becoming highly successful when she gave birth to a brain-damaged child, cut back on touring, moved to my parents' building, and devoted herself to her child. I had never seen her in all the years she had lived there.

I didn't say anything to her. She didn't know me; I don't think she knew my parents well at all. We were caretakers passing in the evening light. Only my job was a short one, unlike hers; my father might be dead by the time I walked back down the stairs with the bundle of magazines and letters.

I put myself in charge of making funeral arrangements.

When I wasn't caring for my father or sleeping, I was figuring out how to dispose of his body. Neither my mother nor my brother wanted this job. I sat at the kitchen table, dialing the phone, noting down casket prices, charges to ship the body. I could do this because I wasn't holding on to him, not at all.

My mother had said my father wanted to be cremated. I mentioned this to one of my parents' friends on the telephone; she said she thought Jews were not allowed to be cremated. It struck me as entirely possible, given our family's ignorance about Judaism, that it had never occurred to my parents to wonder where Jewish law and tradition stood on the question of cremation. My guess was that my father chose cremation because it struck him as less corny; at the same time I was sure that if cremation violated some Jewish principle, he would not want to go through with it. Despite being completely unobservant, he felt indelibly Jewish.

How to find out? My parents didn't belong to any synagogue, so there was no rabbi I could ask. Finally I phoned the rabbi who had recently performed Maury's sister's wedding ceremony and who had impressed me that day with his thoughtfulness. He was the Hillel rabbi at Yale. When I reached him, he said he would be happy to try to advise me.

The rabbi explained to me that the body should decompose into the earth as quickly as possible, with only the flimsiest barriers. Hence it should be wrapped in a linen shroud and placed in a simple pine box. Cremation is not strictly forbidden, but it is generally not done, since it goes against this strong tradition, one which he said he found quite beautiful.

There was a pause. Then he said: But let me ask you, do you know why your father wishes to be cremated? No? Well, I haven't made a formal study of this at all, not in any way, but it is my personal opinion that the wish to be cremated is involved with anger. My own mother wanted to be cremated, and she was a very angry person. Something about the flames. Maybe this is just me, but I feel there is some truth to it.

My mother was sitting on the couch in the living room, hands folded in her lap. My brother was in the bedroom with my father. I asked her, as gently as I could, Why does Dad want to be cremated? Do you know? She screwed up her face as if she were tasting something sour.

I told her the rabbi's theory about anger. Oh no, that's not it, she said. Sidney wanted to be cremated only because he was afraid no one would ever come to visit his grave. He said he couldn't stand the thought of lying alone in one of those huge cemeteries out in the middle of New Jersey with miles and miles of graves and no one ever coming to visit him.

So that was it. He didn't want to be abandoned, anonymous. He was afraid. He'd rather disappear into ashes and smoke. I didn't want him interred out of fear. I wanted to find a way that would please him, if he knew about it, which in some way he would. There had to be a solution. I sat at the kitchen table, my fingers punching the buttons of the phone. I talked to this person and that, and in the end I made an arrangement for him he would have loved.

He is buried in the outskirts of Boston, at the Workmen's Circle Cemetery, for which he was eligible through my mother, who had been brought up a Workmen's Circle child. He's where he should be, buried with the old Yiddish-speaking socialist Jews.

It's a beautiful cemetery. Very small, with woods all around. To get to it, you walk down a long gravelly, bumpy road, like an old farm road. On one side of the road are a parade of small cemeteries, each reserved for a different shul or Jewish organization. They have decorative iron-gated or arched entrances, the ironwork often old and rusty. On the other side of the road are fields and woods; there is a historical marker noting that this was the site of Brook Farm, the early experiment in utopian communal living. Your father would love this, my mother always says when we pass the sign. To be buried near Brook Farm, to be buried in a Workmen's Circle cemetery, in such a beautiful place; he would love it.

Then one of us says, Yeah, if he weren't dead he'd be glad to be buried here, or some such joke, and we laugh.

On his gravestone is carved an open book, for his love of reading, and a bar of the Charlie Parker tune "Now's the Time." On the stone the engraved letters say, Play the Melody, and then there's his name and the year he was born and the year he died.

These days, every morning I take one of the tiny blue pills that have miraculously made my panic attacks extinct. I feel as grateful as any patient with a chronic illness who unexpectedly has found a cure. I know I will have to take these pills forever, but I don't care.

I had despaired of a treatment. Given up all hope. Now, miraculously, the street is just a street, the sidewalk just a sidewalk. Nervousness is only that, not the first inches of a slick slide into panic, falling off the end of the world.

I live in an old wooden house with white curtains blowing at the windows. I have a garden and enough money. I cook well and make dinner every night, as much for myself as for my children and Maury.

I have this paper, typed by my father, part of a letter never sent:

It began last night. I jumped up out of a fevered sleep, still in a frenzy I remembered hearing my voice reading a poem about Yard-bird, my words icicles falling through a limitless black void, each word precise, unadorned, hard as diamonds, crystal clear, fixed as stars, each a signpost pointing back to the heart-stopping terrible beauty of those holy days. The midnight meets on insane rooftops, the unseen hands pulling my coat, the narcotized sandpaper voices, "Hey, Bruz, want some boy? want some girl?" the hysterical stink of my icy sweating armpits, the toilets in gas stations, hotel lobbies, Bickford's, temples where I did my praying, cats folding up like accordions, uttering one last gasp and then dying, and me not here here and Bird blowing a howling wind making divine the leaden love songs of tinny pan alley, his notes full of quivering urgency, the trembling truth of yesterday, today, and fuck tomorrow, the shaman played and paid with this life, we were all naked and on our ass, all my old high fliers were earthbound and life hung from a string of notes.